Physical Activities for Young People With Severe Disabilities

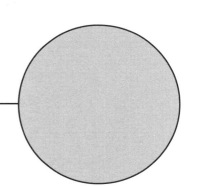

Lindsay K. Canales, MA

Rebecca K. Lytle, PhD

Human
Kinetics

Library of Congress Cataloging-in-Publication Data

Canales, Lindsay, 1980-
  Physical activities for young people with severe disabilities / Lindsay Canales and Rebecca Lytle.
    p. cm.
  Includes bibliographical references.
  ISBN-13: 978-0-7360-9597-6 (soft cover)
  ISBN-10: 0-7360-9597-7 (soft cover)
  1. Learning disabled children--Education--United States. 2. People with disabilities--Education--
United States. 3. Sports administration--United States. I. Lytle, Rebecca K., 1961- II. Title.
  LC4802.C366 2011
  371.91--dc22

                          2010040437

ISBN-10: 0-7360-9597-7 (print)
ISBN-13: 978-0-7360-9597-6 (print)

The Web addresses cited in this text were current as of December 2010, unless otherwise noted.

Acquisitions Editor: Cheri Scott; **Developmental Editor:** Jacqueline Eaton Blakley; **Assistant Editors:** Anne Rumery and Derek Campbell; **Copyeditor:** Patsy Fortney; **Graphic Designer:** Nancy Rasmus; **Graphic Artist:** Yvonne Griffith; **Cover Designer:** Keith Blomberg; **Photographer (cover):** Lindsay K. Canales; **Photographer (interior):** Bruce King/© Human Kinetics; **Photo Asset Manager:** Laura Fitch; **Visual Production Assistant:** Joyce Brumfield; **Photo Production Manager:** Jason Allen; **Art Manager:** Kelly Hendren; **Associate Art Manager:** Alan L. Wilborn; **Printer:** Versa Press

Printed in the United States of America

10 9 8 7 6 5 4 3 2 1

The paper in this book is certified under a sustainable forestry program.

Human Kinetics
Web site: www.HumanKinetics.com

United States: Human Kinetics
P.O. Box 5076
Champaign, IL 61825-5076
800-747-4457
e-mail: humank@hkusa.com

Canada: Human Kinetics
475 Devonshire Road Unit 100
Windsor, ON N8Y 2L5
800-465-7301 (in Canada only)
e-mail: info@hkcanada.com

Europe: Human Kinetics
107 Bradford Road
Stanningley
Leeds LS28 6AT, United Kingdom
+44 (0) 113 255 5665
e-mail: hk@hkeurope.com

Australia: Human Kinetics
57A Price Avenue
Lower Mitcham, South Australia 5062
08 8372 0999
e-mail: info@hkaustralia.com

New Zealand: Human Kinetics
P.O. Box 80
Torrens Park, South Australia 5062
0800 222 062
e-mail: info@hknewzealand.com

E5194

CONTENTS

ACTIVITY FINDER

Activity name	Primary concepts	Secondary concepts	Equipment	Page number
Air Hockey Knockdown	Eye–hand coordination	Aim, force, accuracy	Beanbags, water bottles, table	46
Ball Attack	Eye–hand coordination	Striking, cardiorespiratory endurance	Large therapy ball, pool noodles, tape	48
Balloon Rockets	Muscular strength and cardiorespiratory endurance	Creative movement, locomotor skills, moving in general space	Rocket balloon pump, rocket balloons	24
Balloon Strike	Eye–hand coordination	Striking, visual tracking	Large balloon, string	50
Beach Ball Golf	Eye–hand coordination	Striking; aim, force, accuracy	Pool noodles, beach balls, hula hoops	52
Beanbag Challenge	Balance and flexibility	Prepositional concepts, body part identification	Beanbags	2
Beanbag Shuffleboard	Eye–hand coordination	Aim, force, accuracy	Beanbags, table, tape	54
Body Bowling	Balance and flexibility	Striking	Bowling pins,* mat	4
Body Bubbles	Balance and flexibility	Body part identification, eye–hand coordination	Bubbles, bubble machine (optional)	6
Bubble Dodging	Muscular strength and cardiorespiratory endurance	Chasing, fleeing, dodging; moving in general space; visual tracking	Bubbles, bubble machine (optional)	26
Bubble Wrap Stomp	Moving in general space	Creative movement, rhythm and beat	Bubble wrap, music or drum	84
Circle Bowling	Eye–hand coordination	Rolling; aim, force, accuracy	Bowling pins,* large ball	56
Circle Soccer	Eye–foot coordination	Kicking; aim, force, accuracy	Large ball, chairs	58

*Indicates that alternative equipment options are described in the activity lesson plan.

(continued)

(continued)

Activity name	Primary concepts	Secondary concepts	Equipment	Page number
Climbing Wall	Balance and flexibility	Eye–hand coordination	Various colors of construction paper cut into a variety of shapes, sizes, and textures; tape	8
Cooperative Marble Pass	Eye–hand coordination	Teamwork	Cardboard mailing tubes, marbles*	60
Crazy Cones	Moving in general space	Chasing, fleeing, dodging; movement pathways	Cones,* pool noodles	86
Fill the Basket	Moving in general space	Grasp and release	Yarn balls,* large cones,* hula hoops	88
Follow the Leader Obstacle Course	Moving in general space	Movement pathways, prepositional concepts	Chalk or tape,* cones*	90
Foxtail Golf	Eye–hand coordination	Throwing; aim, force, accuracy	Foxtail,* buckets,* cones	62
Hit the Can	Eye–hand coordination	Throwing; rolling; aim, force, accuracy	Beanbags,* empty cans or bottles	64
Knock It Out	Eye–hand coordination	Rolling; aim, force, accuracy	Beach balls, tape, small balls, bowling ramp (optional)	66
Laser Maze	Muscular strength and cardiorespiratory endurance	Head control, visual tracking	Laser pointer, headband, colored tape, blank wall	28
Mini Baseball	Muscular strength and cardiorespiratory endurance	Eye–hand coordination, striking, moving in general space	Large cone,* large Wiffle ball, hula hoop, poly spot, paddle*	30
Modified Bocce Ball	Eye–hand coordination	Grasp and release; aim, force, accuracy	Marble,* medium-size ball,* cardboard mailing tube	68
Noodle Tag	Moving in general space	Chasing, fleeing, dodging; cardiorespiratory endurance	Pool noodles	92

Activity name	Primary concepts	Secondary concepts	Equipment	Page number
Not in My Backyard!	Muscular strength and cardiorespiratory endurance	Eye–hand coordination; throwing (aim, force, accuracy); striking	Yarn balls,* masking tape* or chalk	32
Parachute Fun	Muscular strength and cardiorespiratory endurance	Prepositional concepts, teamwork	Parachute, yarn balls*	34
Pathway Control	Balance and flexibility	Eye–foot coordination, accuracy	Sidewalk chalk*	14
Ping-Pong Hockey	Muscular strength and cardiorespiratory endurance	Visual tracking	Ping-Pong ball, straws (optional), cardboard,* table	36
Plate Aerobics	Balance and flexibility	Muscular strength, cardiorespiratory endurance	Paper plates	12
Poly Spot Obstacle Course	Muscular strength and cardiorespiratory endurance	Moving in general space	Poly spots, timer (optional)	38
Power Chair Joust	Eye–hand coordination	Striking, moving in general space	Pool noodles, cones, medium-size balls	70
Power Soccer	Muscular strength and cardiorespiratory endurance	Eye–foot coordination, moving in general space	Large therapy ball, cones or nets	40
Rhythm Sticks and Musical Instruments	Moving in general space	Creative movement, rhythm and beat, prepositional concepts	Rhythm sticks,* musical instruments, music, music player	94
Scarves and Ribbon Sticks	Moving in general space	Creative movement, rhythm and beat	Scarves, ribbon sticks,* music, music player	96
Shoot the Tube	Balance and flexibility	Eye–hand and eye–foot coordination	Large therapy ball	16
Sit and Pull	Balance and flexibility	Muscular strength, cardiorespiratory endurance	20-foot (6 m) rope, hook, scooter board (optional)	18

(continued)

Activity name	Primary concepts	Secondary concepts	Equipment	Page number
Sit Down Volleyball	Balance and flexibility	Eye–hand coordination, striking	Beach ball,* approximately 12-foot (3.5 m) rope, two chairs, poly spots	20
Spray Down	Eye–hand coordination	Grasp and release; aim, force, accuracy	Spray bottle, Ping-Pong ball, water bottle*	76
Steal the Chicken	Moving in general space	Chasing, fleeing, dodging; cardiorespiratory endurance	Rubber chicken,* poly spots*	98
Stop and Go!	Moving in general space	Cardiorespiratory endurance, prepositional concepts	Stop and go signal*	100
String Ball	Eye–hand coordination	Crossing the midline	Wiffle ball, string	78
Swing Bowling	Eye–hand coordination	Aim, force, accuracy	20-foot (6 m) rope, playground-size ball, pillowcase, bowling pins,* hook	80
Tail Tag	Moving in general space	Chasing, fleeing, dodging; cardiorespiratory endurance	Ribbon*	102
Team Basketball	Moving in general space	Passing, teamwork, cardiorespiratory endurance	Basketball,* hula hoops,* cones*	104
Tent Pole Jump Rope	Balance and flexibility	Coordination, muscular strength	Collapsible tent pole	10
Therapy Band Resistance Activities	Muscular strength and cardiorespiratory endurance	Flexibility	Therapy bands or tubing	42
Three in a Row!	Eye–hand coordination	Throwing; aim, force, accuracy	Beanbags, hula hoops	72
Throw It; Then Roll It!	Eye–hand coordination	Throwing; rolling; aim, force, accuracy	Yarn balls, beanbags	74
Traffic	Moving in general space	Cardiorespiratory endurance, movement concepts	Visual signs for fast, medium, slow, and stop;* music*	106

INTRODUCTION ⎯⎯⎯⎯⎯⎯⎯⎯⎯⎯○

Physical Activities for Young People With Severe Disabilities was written to help teachers in public school settings provide physical activities for students in grades 6 through 12 who have severe physical disabilities. Such disabilities include cerebral palsy, spina bifida, and other orthopedic impairments that inhibit overall physical functioning. These students might not be able to participate in a general physical education program with their age-level peers or might need additional services in addition to inclusive physical education.

Although written with the needs of the public school teacher in mind, this book is useful to a variety of professionals—adapted physical education specialists, special education teachers, therapeutic recreation specialists, physical education teachers, and others who plan and implement activity programs for young people with severe physical disabilities.

This book presents 50 activities that you can use immediately with your students who have disabilities. The activities make use of common equipment and are easy to prepare for and conduct. They are organized according to the physical skills developed, so it's easy to find the ones that will be most useful for your students. Rather than following a sequence or order, you can choose activities based on an individual student's area of need or to accomplish a particular academic or gross motor goal specified on the student's individualized education program (IEP).

Although the activities in this book specifically target the physical effects of exercise, all lessons are intended to increase the student's psychological well-being as well. It is anticipated that the student outcome of the activities will be increased positive behaviors, self-esteem and confidence, and an increased willingness to interact with those in the general population.

These activities are designed for children and adolescents enrolled in the public school special education system at the secondary level (grades 6 through 12, ages 11 through 17). This age range was selected to support the Individuals with Disabilities Education Act (IDEA), public law 108-466 (2004), which states that physical education is a required service for children and youth between the ages of 0 and 22 who qualify for special education services because of a specific disability or developmental delay.

Because physical activity programs should be based on appropriate content standards, the activities in this book relate to the National Association for Sport and Physical Education (NASPE) content standards. NASPE is a professional organization that sets standards and guidelines for practice in physical education and sport. Its published list of standards for students grades K-12 help define "what a student should know and be able to do as a result of a quality physical education program" (NASPE, 2004, p. 9). The six standards state that a physically educated person:

- **Standard 1:** Demonstrates competency in motor skills and movement patterns needed to perform a variety of physical activities.

- **Standard 2:** Demonstrates understanding of movement concepts, principles, strategies, and tactics as they apply to the learning and performance of physical activities.
- **Standard 3:** Participates regularly in physical activity.
- **Standard 4:** Achieves and maintains a health-enhancing level of physical fitness.
- **Standard 5:** Exhibits responsible personal and social behavior that respects self and others in physical activity settings.
- **Standard 6:** Values physical activity for health, enjoyment, challenge, self-expression, and/or social interaction. (NASPE, 2004, p. 11)

The NASPE standards also provide guidelines for a high-quality physical education program. They stipulate that a student must have the opportunity to learn by having "instructional periods totaling a minimum of 150 minutes per week (elementary) and 225 minutes per week (middle and secondary school)" (NASPE, 2004, p. 5). Because the activities in this book are designed to be carried out in public school settings, we developed them using the NASPE guidelines and standards.

Organization of the Activities

The activities in this book are designed to increase or maintain levels of muscular strength, cardiorespiratory endurance, and flexibility. They are also intended to be positive experiences that enhance self-esteem, self-worth, confidence, and overall psychological well-being. They are grouped into chapters that address four fitness categories: balance and flexibility, muscular strength and cardiorespiratory endurance, eye–hand and eye–foot coordination, and moving in general space. Following are explanations of these categories.

- **Balance and flexibility.** The 10 activities in chapter 1, Balance and Flexibility Activities, focus on increasing or maintaining balance and flexibility. These activities involve extending the upper and lower extremities to reach for an object, maintaining a stretch position or body stance for an extended period of time, or manipulating an object by balancing it appropriately on a specific body part.
- **Muscular strength and cardiorespiratory endurance.** The 10 activities in chapter 2, Muscular Strength and Cardiorespiratory Endurance Activities, focus on overall body strength and cardiorespiratory endurance. These activities involve constant body movement such as walking, running, propelling a wheelchair, and continuously moving the upper or lower extremities. Resistance training activities using equipment such as therapy bands and one's own body weight, as well as activities in which the objective is to maintain movement for a period of time, are all designed to maintain or increase muscular strength and cardiorespiratory endurance.
- **Eye–hand and eye–foot coordination.** The 18 activities in chapter 3, Eye–Hand and Eye–Foot Coordination Activities, involve coordination of the eye to hand as well as the eye to foot. These activities address tracking an

object with the eye in order to contact it with the hand or foot appropriately. Skills that demonstrate eye–hand and eye–foot coordination include striking an object using an implement (e.g., bat, paddle, hockey stick), kicking a ball, and throwing a ball toward a target. When performing these types of skills toward a target, students need to demonstrate appropriate aim, force, and accuracy. In many cases, students who are unable to use their hands in an activity may use their feet. For example, a child with cerebral palsy may be able to move a foot better than a hand to propel an object. For this reason many activities in this chapter can be modified to use the hand or the foot depending on the needs of the student and the goals of the lesson.

- **Moving in general space.** The 12 activities in chapter 4, Moving in General Space Activities, address moving within specified boundaries safely, without bumping into others. Many activities that involve moving in general space allow a student to move around freely while following specific movement cues or prepositions (e.g., *stop, go, under, around, up*). Other skills recognized within this category include chasing, fleeing, and dodging. These movement skills are often seen in cooperative tag games, in which a person must either tag or avoid being tagged by another player.

Each activity in the book is broken down into the following sections:

- **Title.** The title is intended to be a fun and creative name for the activity. It is not intended to describe the goal or purpose of the activity.

- **Primary concept(s).** This section identifies the category of physical fitness the activity addresses. As mentioned, the activities are divided into four fitness categories (balance and flexibility, muscular strength and cardiorespiratory endurance, eye–hand and eye–foot coordination, and moving in general space).

- **Secondary concept(s).** Many of the activities cover multiple skills or movement concepts. This section identifies the secondary skills or movement concepts specifically. Skills include striking, kicking, throwing, catching, rolling, chasing, fleeing, and dodging. The movement concepts include using creative movement patterns; understanding prepositions; and using appropriate aim, force, and accuracy when performing a skill.

- **Activity goal.** This section gives an overview of the general goal of the activity, describing what will be accomplished during the activity, and what the students will have learned by the end of it.

- **Equipment.** The materials needed for conducting the activity are listed in this section. A particular quantity of equipment might not be specified because it may vary depending on the number of students, their skill level, and the space your students will be working in. Because maximizing student participation is so important, you should try to have at least one piece of equipment per student unless students will be working in pairs or small groups. It is also important to provide a variety of equipment options to offer various levels of difficulty, thus maximizing student success (e.g., balls, beach balls, and beanbags for catching). Your role is to determine the most appropriate equipment based on individual student abilities.

- **Setup.** This section addresses what you need to do prior to the lesson, such as setting up the space or facility or organizing the activity.

- **Procedure.** This section describes how to implement the lesson from beginning to end. Included are the exact directions and instructional cues to use to lead the activity.

- **Low variations.** Any activity, as described in the step-by-step procedure section, may not be appropriate for all students. This section offers suggestions for adapting the activity for students who are extremely low functioning and may need modifications to achieve a level of success.

- **High variations.** Some of the activities, as described in the step-by-step procedure section, may be too simple for particular students. This section offers suggestions for adapting the activity for students who are higher functioning and may need modifications to make the activity more challenging.

- **Informal assessment questions.** Assessment is an important tool for ensuring that your students are successful and that they are reaching a level of understanding when performing an activity. In general, assessment should take place before, during, and after the implementation of a physical activity program. It should help you answer important questions pertaining to the student's success. Following are examples of questions you may need to answer:

  - What are the student's current abilities?
  - What types of activities are appropriate for this student?
  - What skills and abilities should be assessed for this student?
  - How effective is the program in meeting the needs of this student?
  - Is the student benefiting from participation in this program?
  - Can instruction be enhanced for this student?
  - What skills and abilities has the student learned through participating in this program?
  - How has the student's quality of life been improved? (Kasser & Lytle, 2005, pp. 74-75)

There are many strategies and tools for assessing students both formally and informally. Formal assessment tools are generally standardized tests with very specific instructions. Informal assessments are much less specific and may include observations, rating scales, student questionnaires, or even reflection questions that check for student understanding. Alternative assessments such as these, which note progress on a daily basis, are more ideal than formal assessments when working with students with severe disabilities.

The assessment questions in this book constitute brief evaluations to help you ensure that your students are meeting the goal or objective of the activity. They are not intended to be overall evaluations of students' performances. A more comprehensive assessment by an adapted physical education specialist is recommended to provide a complete understanding of students' overall gross motor abilities.

Ensuring Safety

People with disabilities typically have unique health and safety issues. Many times students with physical disabilities lack overall strength and endurance in comparison to their age-level peers, which can lead to overexertion and overuse of the body's systems. They may also be more prone to infection or secondary conditions because of their disability or because of particular medications they may be taking.

Because of these medical factors and concerns, you need to take extra precautions when planning for students with disabilities in a physical education setting. Being aware of the environment in terms of safety is crucial. Choosing equipment that you can adapt to meet the needs of your students in regard to texture, size, and weight may be necessary. Also, staying current on training in CPR and knowing the protocol for responding to seizure episodes are important.

You must also understand the individual needs of your students. Looking at their confidential files, which address very specific concerns, is critical in providing a safe learning environment. Consulting with the special education nurse is another way to get important information on the health of individual students. The nurse will have information on the side effects of medications a student is taking, whether the student is allergic to anything, or whether the student has diabetes, a seizure disorder, or asthma. If you have any concerns regarding specific medical alerts as they relate to physical activity, ask for a physician's release for the student to participate in physical activity, and follow your school district's protocols.

Educating students with disabilities about safety and exercise precautions will help them be aware of their personal environment and tolerance for exercise. Until students are able to fully understand the health and safety concerns within a physical education setting, however, they must be closely monitored by professionals who are educated on the necessary precautions and able to supervise their participation in physical activity. For example, a student with latex allergies may not be aware of the types of equipment that may contain latex; thus, you need to be on alert. Specific safety concerns related to the activities in this book are presented throughout. However, trained and qualified personnel must attend to the individual safety considerations for specific students.

Teaching Strategies and Tips

To ensure optimal performance in your exercise intervention programs, you must apply effective teaching strategies. Teaching children and adolescents both functional skills and generalization is very important for increasing their independence and ability to participate in activities of daily living (Brown et al., 2001).

Additional strategies for engaging a student in learning include giving choices and using positive reinforcers (Wolery & Schuster, 1997). More specifically, research shows that using short verbal and physical cues, increasing the time a student is engaged in the skill, and individualizing (differentiating) instruction (DePauw, 1996) create a positive learning environment in physical education.

Increasing opportunities for children and adolescents to participate in physical activities during the school day is beneficial. Teaching physical education as part of the classroom curriculum is mandated for children and adolescents with a disability under IDEA (2004) and is supported by both international and national organizations that have set out recommended guidelines for physical activity. Ultimately, the goal is to increase overall functioning and quality of life for all people, including those with severe physical disabilities.

Educating and assessing students with severe disabilities in a school setting can be very difficult (Kauffman & Krouse, 1981; Kleinert & Kearns, 1999; Meyer, Eichinger, & Park-Lee, 1987). In many situations, students that make up this population are not able to grasp concepts or reach the same level of knowledge as their age-level peers (Brown et al., 2001). For this reason, alternative approaches to teaching are necessary to ensure that students with disabilities gain knowledge at their optimal levels. Educators also need to consider what is important to teach students who may not have the physical or mental ability to demonstrate complete knowledge and understanding of the core subject areas of math, English, science, and history. Much research in special education concludes that teaching low-functioning students functional skills and generalization may be the most appropriate form of public education (Brown et al., 2001).

Following are some strategies that research has shown to be effective when teaching students with disabilities:

- Keep the student engaged in a task for a significant period of time.
- Present the material in a clear and organized manner.
- Present the information verbally.
- Present the information using physical cues such as demonstrations.
- Keep both verbal and physical cues short and simple to help keep the student focused on the task, and to avoid overwhelming him or her.
- Provide the student with quality feedback.
- Use strategies to increase motivation, such as giving the student choices, organizing the delivery in a way that interests the student, and using positive reinforcers consistently.
- Allow for functional outcomes that are important in both present and future environments.
- Have the student perform in multiple settings to generalize the learning.

Each activity presented in this book can be altered to fit the needs of your students as well as the environment and equipment that you have access to. Use the following teacher-tested tips as you incorporate the activities into your own classes:

- **Vary the equipment.** Varying the equipment (e.g., changing the size, weight, or texture) can increase the success rate of your students without changing the goal or objective of the activity. Changing the amount of equipment can speed up (more equipment) or slow down (less equipment) the pace of the activity. Homemade equipment can be very cheap and simple to make. Yarn balls, nylon Frisbees, water bottles, aluminum cans, and coffee creamer containers are all examples of homemade equipment that can be used in the activities in this book.

- **Adapt to your environment.** Most of the activities in this book can be conducted in multiple environments with minor changes. If you are carrying out an activity in a confined space, you can use fewer rules, take away some of the equipment, or change the equipment to something lighter that will move more slowly (e.g., a balloon). If you are in a large area, break up the students so that multiple activities are occurring at a time (i.e., a circuit) or so that all students are performing the desired activity at one time. This keeps students active and avoids having some standing or sitting around while waiting for a turn.

- **Use location indicators.** Using an object or a marker to indicate the location you would like students to sit at, stand on, or move to is very helpful. Poly spots, which are pliable circles, can be very useful in helping students follow directions and keeping them focused on the task. You may also use lines on the ground, masking tape to create a design, sidewalk chalk, or laminated construction paper cut into shapes to designate a desired location (e.g., if you would like students to sit in a circle, place the location indicators on the ground in the shape of a circle; then ask the students to move to the circle area, find a spot, and sit down).

- **Use verbal and visual cues.** A cue is a word, phrase, picture, or demonstration that helps describe the skill you are teaching. Using cues that are short and simple (one word or one motion) helps students focus on the task and avoids overwhelming them with instruction. For example, if you are teaching an overhand throw, focus on having students place the ball or beanbag by their ear before releasing it. Once they are able to do that consistently, move on to the next overhand throwing cue: stepping with the opposite foot forward.

- **Be flexible about time.** The duration of a lesson may vary based on the level of the students and their overall success rate. It is important to keep in mind that repetition is good for students with disabilities and that they may require multiple attempts to reach a level of understanding. Never give up on your first try!

- **Keep the activity at eye level.** Many activities are more successful for students with severe physical disabilities when they occur at eye level. Performing activities at a table or using targets on a wall may help students have a more visual understanding of the activity and may encourage them to get more involved. This strategy may also allow students to manipulate an object more successfully. For example, a student who uses a wheelchair, crutches, or a walker for the majority of the school day may have difficulty participating in activities such as bowling that require manipulating an object with two hands. Bringing the bowling activity to a table where the student can better manipulate the object may increase the student's success rate.

- **Use music.** Music and musical instruments have many uses when teaching physical activities. Movement music that verbalizes specific tasks may get students involved and encourage them to follow directions. Finding music with a simple beat that students can follow by waving a ribbon stick in the air or tapping sticks can be very effective as well. You can also play music as a start and stop signal or use music with different beats as students move in space (slow, medium, fast).

- **Emphasize cause and effect.** Activities and equipment that demonstrate cause and effect can be very rewarding for students with severe physical disabilities. They enjoy, for example, watching bowling pins or water bottles fall over when contacted. Switches are also popular with this population (e.g., when they hit the switch, a light turns on). Incorporating cause and effect may maintain students' interest in the activity and can help them understand the goal they are working toward.

- **Establish and maintain routines.** Establishing a routine is very valuable for classroom management. Having a regular warm-up routine, a location students always go to, or an icon they follow every time they begin an activity can help keep them focused and on task. Closing with the same routine is useful as well. Conducting a regular cool-down routine, having students place the equipment in a routine location, or closing with questions that check for understanding are effective ways to transition them to the next task in their school day.

- **Focus on or change movement patterns.** Movement patterns are the skills required to perform an activity or take part in a sport. For example, in the game of basketball, players must be able to dribble, pass, catch, shoot, run, slide, and change direction quickly. Changing the movement patterns within an activity, or focusing on only one or two movements, can increase students' success when participating in modified games or activities. For example, in basketball, perhaps students do not have to dribble, only pass and catch to move the ball, or walk rather than run. Use easier or fewer skills to make a task easier and use more complete movements and increase the number of skills to perform to make a task more difficult.

Conclusion

Finding appropriate physical activities for students with severe physical disabilities can be challenging for any teacher. As a result, such students often end up in passive roles during physical education. The intention of this book is to provide a host of activities that can be connected to both appropriate grade-level standards and IEP goals and objectives. Increased engagement in physical activity will result in enhanced fitness, enjoyment, and quality of life for your students with disabilities.

ACKNOWLEDGMENTS

We would like to thank, first and foremost, the children and families who have taught us so much over the years. Second, we would like to thank Mesa Vista School and all of the teachers and models who helped bring this book to life. Finally, we would like to thank the Northern California Adapted Physical Education Consortium of teachers for all the ideas and activities collaboratively developed over the years, which contributed greatly to the content of this book.

In loving memory of Jesse Kohen, whose energy and enthusiasm touched the lives of many children.

CHAPTER 1

Balance and Flexibility Activities

The 10 activities in this chapter focus on increasing or maintaining balance and flexibility. These activities involve extending the upper and lower extremities to reach for an object, maintaining a stretch position or body stance for an extended period of time, or manipulating an object by balancing it appropriately on a specific body part.

Beanbag Challenge

Primary Concepts
Balance and flexibility

Secondary Concepts
Prepositional concepts; body part identification

Activity Goal
To balance a beanbag on specified body parts while maintaining balance.

Equipment
Beanbags (one per student)

Setup
Arrange the students in a circle and give each a beanbag.

Procedure
1. Have each student hold the beanbag in a still position.
2. Name and demonstrate a movement while the students mirror your movements. Try the following movements, which are listed in order from easiest to hardest:
   - Balance beanbag on head; then balance beanbag on arm; then lift the arm up and down.
   - Balance beanbag on tummy.
   - Balance beanbag on ear.
   - Balance beanbag on back.
   - Balance beanbag on shoulder.
   - Balance beanbag on one knee, then the other knee.
   - Balance beanbag on head and turn in a circle.
   - Balance beanbag on foot; then lift foot up and down.
   - Throw beanbag up and catch it.
   - From behind, throw beanbag through legs and catch it.
   - Throw beanbag up, clap once, and catch it.

Low Variations
- Use a hand-over-hand technique (physically assist).
- Use basic, one-part cues that focus only on the body part (e.g., "Beanbag on head").
- Allow students to use the other hand to balance the beanbag.

High Variations
- Name the beanbag challenge without demonstrating it.
- Have students call out the cues.
- Play the beanbag challenge as a Simon says game.

Informal Assessment Questions

- Is the student able to hold the beanbag on the specified body parts?
- Is the student able to recognize body parts either verbally or physically?

Suggested Music

- Greg & Steve, *Kids in Motion: Beanbag Boogie I, Beanbag Boogie II*
- Greg & Steve, *Kids in Action: Beanie Bag Dance*

Body Bowling

Primary Concepts
Balance and flexibility

Secondary Concept
Striking

Activity Goal
To demonstrate flexibility by using the body to knock down bowling pins or other upright objects.

Equipment
- Bowling pins or light objects that can be knocked over, such as coffee creamer containers, 1-quart (1 L) milk cartons, empty water bottles, or tin cans
- Approximately a 10-foot (3 m) mat or soft surface for each student

Setup
Place the mat on the floor in an open space with no obstacles (an open carpet area will work as well). Set up the bowling pins all around the designated mat area.

Procedure
1. Have students lie on the mat or floor surface.
2. On your signal, students extend their bodies in all directions, knocking down all of the pins surrounding them.

Low Variations
- Position the pins closer to students so they don't have to reach as far to knock them down.
- Allow students to sit in chairs and use pool noodles or paddles to knock down the pins.

High Variations
- Position the pins farther from the students so they must reach to knock them down.
- Have students perform log rolls, propelling their bodies into the pins to knock them down.
- Arrange the pins farther apart on a hard surface. Have students maneuver themselves on scooter boards to knock down the pins.

Informal Assessment Questions
- Is the student knocking over the pins using a body part?
- Is the student able to knock down at least one of the standing pins?

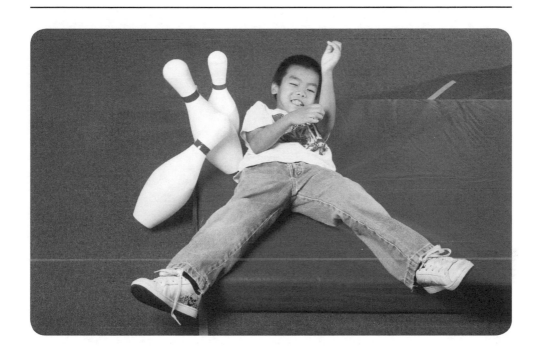

Body Bubbles

Primary Concepts
Balance and flexibility

Secondary Concepts
Body part identification; eye–hand coordination

Activity Goal
To pop bubbles using specified body parts.

Equipment
Bubbles (store bought or homemade, large or small) (You can find a recipe for homemade bubbles at http://bubbleblowers.com/homemade.html.)

Setup
Find a large area free of obstacles.

> ### SAFETY TIP
> Do not conduct this activity on a tile or gym floor. Soap suds will make the floors very slippery.

Procedure
1. Position the students approximately 5 feet (1.5 m) or more from the person blowing the bubbles (or bubble machine).
2. Have one person call out a body part.
3. Have the person blowing the bubbles blow one set of bubbles (approximately 10) while the students attempt to pop them using the body part that was called out.
4. Once the bubbles disappear, repeat the procedure.

Low Variations
- Have the person blowing the bubbles blow one at a time.
- Have students track the bubbles with their eyes or head only.
- Use large bubbles only.
- Have pictures of body parts on task cards and have students pick up a task card and pop the bubbles using the pictured body part.

High Variations
- Increase the speed of the bubble blowing.
- Allow students to blow the bubbles or call out the body parts.
- Have students count how many bubbles they popped using the specified body part.

Informal Assessment Questions

- Is the student able to identify body parts?
- Is the student able to contact the bubble using the specified body part?

Climbing Wall

Primary Concepts
Balance and flexibility

Secondary Concept
Eye–hand coordination

Activity Goal
To maneuver across a designated space while maintaining balance.

Equipment
Colored construction paper cut out into a variety of shapes, sizes, and textures; tape (For longevity and multiple use, laminate the shapes.)

Setup
Tape the colored shapes randomly (i.e., at high, medium, and low levels) along a wall that is approximately 20 feet long and 7 feet high (6 m by 2 m) and on the ground where the wall and the floor meet.

Procedure
1. Have students begin at one end of the wall.
2. Call out cues for movement on the climbing wall—for example, "With your left foot, step on a red heart on the ground, and with your right hand, find a blue star on the wall."
3. Continue to call out cues until students have made it to the end of the climbing wall.
4. If multiple students are participating, have them spread out along the climbing wall so they are starting at different locations.

Low Variations
- Use shapes only on the wall or only on the ground.
- Call out only single-part cues (colors or shapes only).
- Do not designate a hand (right or left).

High Variations
- Make cues more complex (e.g., "Right hand on blue star").
- Have students call out the cues.
- Arrange shapes so they are more difficult to find.

Informal Assessment Questions
- Is the student able to identify shapes, colors, and textures?
- Is the student able to move from one shape to another appropriately?

Tent Pole Jump Rope

Primary Concepts
Balance and flexibility

Secondary Concepts
Coordination; muscular strength

Activity Goal
To experience the rhythm and movement associated with jumping rope by jumping, stepping, or rolling over a tent pole turned as a jump rope.

Equipment
Collapsible tent pole (to be used as a jump rope)

Setup
Connect the tent pole so that it creates a solid line.

Procedure
1. Have two adults or able students hold each end of the tent pole allowing it to bend slightly so that the center of the pole is touching the ground (this is the jump rope).
2. Have the student stand in the center as in traditional jump rope.
3. Have the helpers turn the pole as in jump rope while the student jumps, steps, or rolls over the pole at the appropriate time. (The tent pole is a great tool for jump rope because it moves much slower than a traditional jump rope does.)

Low Variations
- Decrease the speed of the pole.
- Have the helpers pause when the pole hits the ground so the student can react by jumping, stepping, or rolling over it.
- Cue the student when it is time to jump.

High Variations
- Increase the speed of the pole.
- Count how many times student can jump the pole consecutively.
- Sing a jump rope rhyme. (Rhymes can be found at www.gameskidsplay. net/Jump_Rope_ryhmes/index.htm.)
- Use a standard jump rope.

Informal Assessment Questions
- Is the student able to jump, step, or roll over the pole at the appropriate time?
- Is the student able to jump over the pole consecutively?

Plate Aerobics

Primary Concepts
Balance and flexibility

Secondary Concepts
Muscular strength; cardiorespiratory endurance

Activity Goal
To perform movement exercises using paper plates while maintaining balance and control.

Equipment
Waxed paper plates (one or two per student)

Setup
Arrange the students in a circle (use spot indicators if desired) on a carpeted surface.

Procedure
1. Have students begin by standing with the right foot on one paper plate and legs shoulder-width apart.
2. Have them put their body weight on the left leg while sliding the right leg out (away from the body) and back in.
3. Now have students slide the right foot (paper plate) forward and backward.
4. Have students switch feet (the paper plate is now under the left foot), and repeat.
5. Once students get the hang of sliding one paper plate using their foot, give them a second paper plate and have them place it under the opposite foot.
6. Now have students move both feet out and in; then one foot forward and the other backward, and switch.
7. Play music and have students dance and move in general space using the paper plates for leg movement. Cue the students with tips for moving in general space:
   - Look for open spaces.
   - Watch for others.

Low Variations
- Have students use their hands instead of their feet. Have them sit with their hands on a table in front of them. They can move their hands out and in, forward and backward.
- Hold students' hands for balance and support.

High Variations

- Have student move across the room by standing sideways, moving their leading foot out, then bringing the following foot in, and repeating the sequence until they reach the opposite side of the room.
- Have students create a dance or a movement sequence using the paper plates.
- Have students use paper plates on both hands and feet.

Informal Assessment Questions

- Is the student able to maintain balance when using the paper plates?
- Is the student able to move for a specified period of time while using the paper plates?

Pathway Control

Primary Concepts
Balance and flexibility

Secondary Concepts
Eye–foot coordination; accuracy

Activity Goal
To propel a wheelchair or scooter board in control on a specified pathway.

Equipment
Sidewalk chalk or tape (can also use cones or mats to mark a pathway)

Setup
Mark a pathway using two parallel lines approximately 5 feet (1.5 m) apart on the ground using the chalk or tape. You can make the pathway simple or complex depending on the students' functional level.

Procedure
1. Have students start at one end of the pathway.
2. On your signal, students propel their wheelchairs or scooter boards along the pathway, trying to stay within the parallel lines and get to the other end.

Low Variations
- Have students focus on keeping only one wheel within the pathway.
- Make the pathway very basic and wide.
- Push students while they verbalize direction and speed.

High Variations
- Make the pathway narrower.
- Make the pathway design more complex, or have students roll backward through it.
- Have students use scooter boards.
- Have students count the number of times they veer out of the pathway lines. Then have them try to decrease that number.
- Time students through the course and challenge them to beat their time.

Informal Assessment Questions
- Is the student able to follow a floor pattern while maintaining balance?
- Is the student able to stay within the lines all the way to the end of the pathway?

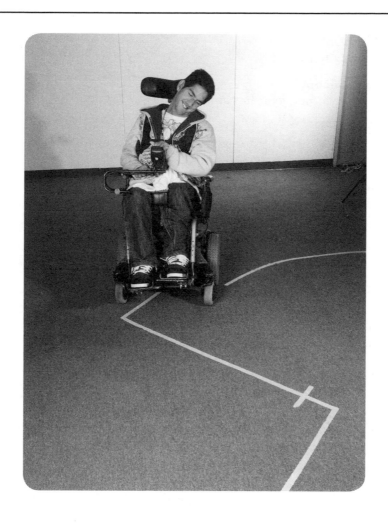

Shoot the Tube

Primary Concepts
Balance and flexibility

Secondary Concepts
Eye–hand and eye–foot coordination

Activity Goal
To roll a large therapy ball through a designated area without the ball being blocked by an opposing student.

Equipment
Large therapy ball

Setup
Use a large playing area free of obstacles (at least 25 ft, or 7.6 m, long) with a blank wall within arm's length of the entire 25-foot area.

Procedure

1. Two students are needed to carry out this activity. Students are in wheel-chairs or in chairs.
2. Position the students approximately 5 feet or 1.5 meters (a little more than arm's length) from the blank wall, facing each other, approximately 25 feet (7.5 m) apart.
3. One student begins with the therapy ball and, on your signal, rolls the ball forward, trying to get it past the other student who is trying to block the ball. Students may use any part of their body to roll and block the ball.
4. Have students alternate offensive (rolling the ball) and defensive (blocking the ball) positions.

Low Variations

- Have students use implements to block the ball.
- Have students use their wheelchairs to block the ball.
- Have the students play at table level. The object is to stop the ball from rolling off the table.

High Variations

- Position students farther than 5 feet (1.5 m) from the wall.
- Have students who can play out of a wheelchair begin in a kneeling position.
- Extend the distance between the students.

The object is to shoot the ball between the chair and the wall. A passed ball scores!

Informal Assessment Questions

- Is the student able to move the therapy ball forward?
- Is the student able to stop the ball from rolling by using the body or an implement?

Sit and Pull

Primary Concepts
Balance and flexibility

Secondary Concepts
Muscular strength; cardiorespiratory endurance

Activity Goal
To hold on to a rope and pull oneself forward as quickly as possible.

Equipment
Rope approximately 20 feet (6 m) long; sturdy fence, hook, or basketball pole on which to secure the rope; scooter board (if appropriate) or wheelchair

Setup
Tie one end of the rope securely to a sturdy fence, hook, or basketball pole no more than 5 feet (1.5 m) from the ground. Lay the rope out straight. Set up multiple ropes for multiple students.

Procedure
1. Have students hold on to the loose end of the rope with two hands. They should be sitting either in a wheelchair or on a scooter board (if appropriate).
2. On your signal, students pull themselves (hand over hand) to the end of the rope as quickly as possible.

Low Variations
- Have students hold on to the rope as you move them around.
- Assist using a hand-over-hand technique.
- Push the chair or board to assist the students while they pull themselves along the rope (hand over hand).

High Variations
- Have two or more students race.
- Have students propel themselves backward until the rope is taut.

Informal Assessment Questions
- Is the student pulling toward the desired location using a hand-over-hand motion?
- Is the student able to balance on the scooter board or in the wheelchair while holding on to the rope?

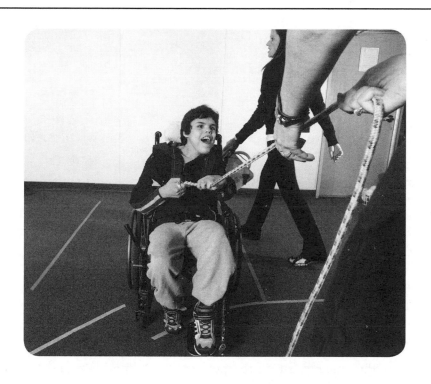

Sit Down Volleyball

Primary Concepts
Balance and flexibility

Secondary Concepts
Eye–hand coordination; striking

Activity Goal
To strike a beach ball over a net using the hands or head while maintaining a seated position.

Equipment
Beach ball or large balloon (a punching balloon works well); rope approximately 12 feet (3.5 m) long; two chairs or objects on which to secure the rope; poly spots (one per student) or markers to indicate where students will be positioned during the activity

Setup
Tie each end of the rope to a chair. This will be your volleyball net (make sure it's not too high off the ground). Place poly spots or marks evenly on both sides of the net (rope) to indicate where students should sit.

Procedure
1. Have the students sit on the poly spots. Divide high- and low-skilled students evenly on each side of the net.
2. Use the cues "Two hands above your head so I know you're ready," and "Keep your eyes on the ball." Students strike the ball forward using both hands to propel the ball over the net (allow students to use their heads).
3. Allow students to hit the ball multiple times on one side of the net before it goes over.
4. If the ball touches the ground, allow a student to throw it over the net to begin the volley again.

Low Variations
- Allow students to catch the ball.
- Allow students to push the ball off their laps or lap trays while another student on the team strikes it before it hits the ground.
- Serve the ball yourself.
- Have students sit in a circle and volley to each other.
- Allow the ball to bounce between strikes.

This game may be played cooperatively with students counting how many times they can hit the ball before it touches the ground.

High Variations

- Count how many times students can strike the ball before it touches the ground.
- Allow students to serve the ball over the net.
- Use traditional volleyball rules (e.g., three hits before the ball must reach the other side of the net).

Informal Assessment Questions

- Is the student able to contact the beach ball using the hands or head?
- Is the student able to maintain a seated position for the duration of the activity?

CHAPTER 2

Muscular Strength and Cardiorespiratory Endurance Activities

The 10 activities in this chapter focus on overall body strength and cardiorespiratory endurance. These activities involve constant body movement such as walking, running, propelling a wheelchair, and continuously moving the upper or lower extremities. Resistance training using equipment such as therapy bands and one's own body weight, as well as activities in which the objective is to maintain movement for a period of time, are all designed to maintain or increase muscular strength and cardiorespiratory endurance.

Balloon Rockets

Primary Concepts
Muscular strength and cardiorespiratory endurance

Secondary Concepts
Creative movement; locomotor skills; moving in general space

Activity Goal
To move through space quickly, toward a designated location, before the balloon touches the ground.

Equipment
Rocket balloon pump (you may want more than one); rocket balloons

- Order rocket balloon sets at www.rocketballoons.com.
- Rocket balloons are also available at Target stores.

Setup
Find an open play area free of obstacles.

Procedure
1. Have the students gather at one end of the play area.
2. Blow up a balloon using the balloon pump; then, on a signal, launch the balloon while the students move across the play area to the other side (or to a designated area). The students must reach the location before the balloon touches the ground.
3. Call out various ways to move to the other side of the play area before the balloon touches the ground (e.g., "Hold one hand in the air," "Make an animal noise," "Count by 5s," "Balance a beanbag on your head," "Gallop," "Run," "Jump," "Slide," "Move like an animal," "Turn your wheelchair around," "Follow another person," "Mirror someone else's movements").

Low Variations
- Have students track the balloon with their eyes or fingers.
- Move students' wheelchairs across the play area.
- Have students chase the balloon.

High Variations
- Have students guess where the balloon will go.
- Discuss the concepts of levels and directions.
- Have students use more complex locomotor movements.
- Have students try to catch the balloon before it touches the ground.

The students are frozen; when the balloons fly away, they will try to catch them.

Informal Assessment Questions

- Is the student moving toward the designated location?
- Is the student performing the specified movement?

Bubble Dodging

Primary Concepts
Muscular strength and cardiorespiratory endurance

Secondary Concepts
Chasing, fleeing, dodging; moving in general space; visual tracking

Activity Goal
To keep bubbles from touching the body by blowing them away, striking them with an implement, or dodging them.

Equipment
Homemade or store-bought bubbles (You can find a recipe for homemade bubbles at http://bubbleblowers.com/homemade.html.)

Setup
Find a large area free of obstacles.

> **SAFETY TIP**
>
> Do not conduct this activity on a tile or gym floor. Soap suds will make the floors very slippery.

Procedure
1. Position the students approximately 5 feet (1.5 m) or more from the person blowing the bubbles (or bubble machine).
2. Have someone blow one set of bubbles (approximately 10) while the students attempt to blow, strike with an implement (a paddle works well), or dodge the bubbles by maneuvering their bodies or wheelchairs. You can give the students these three options or specify which you want them to use based on their functional levels.
3. Once the bubbles disappear, repeat the procedure.

Low Variations
- Have students blow a single bubble at a time.
- Have students track the bubbles with their eyes or head only.
- Use large bubbles only.

High Variations
- Increase the speed of the bubble blowing.
- Allow students to blow the bubbles.
- Specify the dodging technique you would like the students to use. For example, moving to the right, moving to the left, or ducking under the bubble.

Informal Assessment Questions

- Is the student able to avoid getting hit by the bubbles?
- How many bubbles did the student avoid?

Laser Maze

Primary Concepts
Muscular strength and cardiorespiratory endurance

Secondary Concepts
Head control; visual tracking

Activity Goal
To follow a pattern or maze using the head to direct a laser light.

Equipment
Laser pointer; headband (to hold laser pointer to head; can also use a headlamp or clip-on light); tape (colored)

Setup
Create a pattern on a blank wall using tape (e.g., parallel lines moving horizontally along the wall to create a maze, a design, or a shape). Attach the laser light to a headband.

Procedure
1. Place the laser pointer on a student's head in the "on" position.
2. Have the student face the wall that has the pattern on it.
3. Have the student use head control to follow the pattern from left to right by keeping the laser point steady between the parallel lines.

Low Variations
- Create a very simple wall design using large shapes. Have the student hold the laser point on one shape using head control.
- Assist the student in maneuvering the laser.
- Make the parallel line design very wide.

High Variations
- Create a more complex design such as a maze.
- Have students race to see who can get through the pattern the quickest moving the laser point from left to right while keeping the point between the lines.
- Allow students to create the wall pattern or verbalize how they would like the design to look.

Informal Assessment Questions
- Is the student able to move the laser from point A to point B?
- Is the student able to keep the laser pointed between the lines?

The student moves his head to move the laser point along the zigzag pathway on the wall.

Mini Baseball

Primary Concepts
Muscular strength and cardiorespiratory endurance

Secondary Concepts
Eye–hand coordination; striking; moving in general space

Activity Goal
To strike a ball using an implement and run to a base before the fielder reaches a designated location.

Equipment
Milk crate or extra large cone (to use as a batting tee); large Wiffle ball; hula hoop; poly spot or other type of spot (to use for a base); pool noodle or lollipop paddle (to use for striking)

Setup
Find a large play area free of obstacles. At one end set up the milk crate or cone as the batting tee. Approximately 20 feet (6 m) in front and to the right of the milk crate, place the poly spot or marker to indicate first base (set up like a baseball diamond). In the center of the play area set the hula hoop on the ground.

Procedure
1. Designate one batter; the rest of the students are fielders.
2. Have the batter face the batting tee.
3. Place the Wiffle ball on the batting tee.
4. Have the batter swing the pool noodle or lollipop paddle to hit the Wiffle ball off the batting tee.
5. When the ball is hit forward, the batter places the "bat" on the floor and moves to the designated base.
6. The fielder's job is to retrieve the ball and try to get inside the hula hoop with the ball in hand before the batter gets to the base.
7. Rotate students so everyone has the opportunity to be both a batter and a fielder.

Low Variations
- Batters can push the ball from their laps to indicate a hit.
- Use a larger ball (beach ball or large balloon).
- Assist fielders by placing the ball on their laps for them to take to the hula hoop.

High Variations
- Pitch the ball to the batter.
- Use multiple bases (first, second, third, home).
- Use more traditional baseball rules.

Informal Assessment Questions

- Is the batter striking the ball off the tee and running to the base consistently?
- Is the fielder retrieving the ball and moving toward the hula hoop consistently?

Not in My Backyard!

Primary Concepts
Muscular strength and cardiorespiratory endurance

Secondary Concepts
Eye–hand coordination; throwing (aim, force, accuracy); striking

Activity Goal
To throw objects into the opposite team's area, while keeping the objects out of one's own team's designated area.

Equipment
Yarn balls or small, lightweight objects; masking tape or cones (inside); chalk (outside)

Setup
Use the masking tape, cones, or chalk to mark a line directly through the center of the large playing area. Place half of the yarn balls on one side of the line and the other half on the opposite side.

Procedure
1. Arrange the students so that half are on one side of the designated line and half are on the other.
2. On your signal ("Go," music, a whistle), students pick up the yarn balls and throw them across the line into the opposite team's "yard." The balls are simultaneously being thrown back and forth across the line.
3. On your second signal, the students stop throwing and gather the balls in their designated areas. If appropriate, have them count the balls to determine which side has more.

Low Variations
- Have higher-skilled players hand the balls to lower-skilled players so that they can throw.
- Allow students to drop the balls or push them from their laps over the line.
- Have students use pool noodles to strike the balls over the line.
- Allow students to pass objects to players on their own team.

High Variations
- Place targets in the yard for the students to hit with the balls they throw.
- Have higher-skilled students hand the balls to lower-skilled students to throw at the targets.
- Have the students count the balls on their side at the end.
- Have students try to catch the balls being thrown by the opposite team before they hit the ground.

Informal Assessment Questions

- Is the student able to retrieve the balls independently or with assistance?
- Is the student throwing balls in the appropriate direction?

Parachute Fun

Primary Concepts
Muscular strength and cardiorespiratory endurance

Secondary Concepts
Prepositional concepts; teamwork

Activity Goal
To move the parachute as a group following movement cues.

Equipment
Parachute (at least 12 ft, or 3.6 m, in diameter); yarn balls or lightweight balls or objects

Setup
Lay the parachute out flat on the ground in a large play area.

Procedure
1. Have the students sit or stand (whichever is appropriate) on the outside of the parachute and hold on with both hands (you can attach the parachute to a wheelchair if necessary).
2. Call out specific directions to students, as follows:
   - Make little waves (shake parachute lightly and slowly).
   - Make big waves (shake parachute hard and fast).
   - Lift up high, count "1, 2, 3," and then pull the parachute down quickly.
   - Place a yarn ball on the parachute and have students repeat the preceding action and watch it fly.
3. Have students stand, sit, or lie on top of the parachute one at a time. Ask each student on the parachute if he or she would like the group to make big waves or small waves. The class then shakes the parachute accordingly while the student moves around on the parachute. Repeat with each participant.
4. Have students stand, sit, or lie under the parachute one at a time while the group moves the parachute. Use the same cues as when students were on top of the parachute.

Low Variations
- Have students use hand loops for a better grip.
- Attach a band to hand loops on the parachute for a longer grip.
- Assist students in moving the parachute.

High Variations

- Play the game, What's popping in the kitchen?
  - Half the students hold the parachute and the other half stand 1 foot (30 cm) behind the ones holding the parachute.
  - Place yarn balls on the parachute.
  - The students holding the parachute move the parachute, causing the balls to come off.
  - The students off the parachute retrieve the balls and throw them back on the parachute.
  - Have students change positions.
- Use direction cues for those holding the parachute (e.g., "1, 2, 3, up!", "1, 2, 3, down!").

Informal Assessment Questions

- Is the student able to maintain a grip on the parachute?
- Is the student able to follow prepositional cues to move the parachute with the group?

Ping-Pong Hockey

Primary Concepts
Muscular strength and cardiorespiratory endurance

Secondary Concept
Visual tracking

Activity Goal
To propel a Ping-Pong ball through a designated goal by blowing.

Equipment
Ping-Pong ball; one straw per student (if applicable); cardboard (e.g., from shoe boxes or gift boxes); table or flat surface

Setup
Line the edges of the flat surface (table) with the cardboard (this creates a boundary so that the Ping-Pong ball does not fall off the edges). Leave the ends of the table open. These are the goals.

Procedure
1. Place the Ping-Pong ball in the middle of the play area.
2. Have students blow the ball forward (using straws if necessary) and try to get it to fall into the goal (i.e., off the end of the table).

Low Variations
- Allow just one student to play at a time, trying to propel the ball with a straw across the table so that it falls into the goal.
- Hold the straw for the student.
- Don't use a straw at all and allow students to use their hands, an object, or a ball pump that blows out air.

High Variations
- Have two students play against each other trying to get the ball into the goal of the opposite player.
- Set up cardboard boxes throughout the play area as obstacles.
- Keep score.

Informal Assessment Questions
- Is the student able to propel the Ping-Pong ball forward using a blowing method?
- Is the student able to keep blowing to get the Ping-Pong ball to the appropriate goal?

Poly Spot Obstacle Course

Primary Concepts
Muscular strength and cardiorespiratory endurance

Secondary Concept
Moving in general space

Activity Goal
To maneuver oneself to find poly spots in the appropriate number sequence (1, 2, 3, 4...) as quickly as possible.

Equipment
Poly spots with numbers on them (1 to 10 or higher) or durable number cards; timer (optional)

Setup
Scatter the poly spots randomly in the play area.

Procedure
1. Have the students maneuver around the play area finding the poly spots in sequence (1, 2, 3, 4 . . .).
2. As students find the appropriate numbers, they turn the poly spots over so that the numbers are no longer visible and then move on to find the next number in the sequence.
3. Have the students find 10 poly spots (or more) in sequence as quickly as possible.

Low Variations
- Do not time the students.
- Use fewer poly spots.
- Assist students in locating the appropriate numbers using verbal or visual cues.

High Variations
- Use more numbers, or use multiples (e.g., 5s, 10s).
- Have the students perform an exercise when they reach certain numbers; for example, when they get to number 5, they must perform five jumping jacks before moving to number 6.
- Have the students perform specified locomotor skills (e.g., skip, gallop, jump) around the play area while they are looking for poly spots.

Informal Assessment Questions

- Is the student able to maneuver through the poly spot sequence safely?
- Is the student able to sequence the numbers correctly?

Power Soccer

Primary Concepts
Muscular strength and cardiorespiratory endurance

Secondary Concepts
Eye–foot coordination; moving in general space

Activity Goal
To push a large therapy ball into a designated goal, while positioned in a wheelchair.

Equipment
Large therapy ball; cones or two nets to designate soccer goals and cones or lines for boundaries

Setup
On a 50-yard (46 m) field (or smaller) free of obstacles, set up a goal at each end. Ensure that the therapy ball is an appropriate size that allows the student to propel it on the ground by using the front of the wheelchair. If the student's wheelchair is too high to contact the ball, connect a piece of cardboard to the front of the wheelchair.

SAFETY TIP
Ensure a safe learning environment by monitoring this activity well. Students must understand how to participate safely.

Procedure
1. Divide the students into two teams.
2. Explain to the students which goal they are trying to score on.
3. Start with the ball in the middle of the play area, and determine which team begins with the ball (i.e., the kickoff).
4. Each team attempts to push the ball across the goal line using only their wheelchairs. Once one team scores, repeat the kickoff.

Low Variations
- Create a rule that all students on the team must contact the ball before shooting at the designated goal.
- Make the play area smaller.
- Use multiple soccer balls.

High Variations
- Have students play designated positions as in traditional soccer (forward, midfielder, defender, and goalie).
- Make the play area larger.

Here the wall area serves as the goal.

Informal Assessment Questions

- Is the student able to move the ball toward the team's goal?
- Is the student able to push the ball appropriately using the wheelchair?

Therapy Band Resistance Activities

Primary Concepts
Muscular strength and cardiorespiratory endurance

Secondary Concept
Flexibility

Activity Goal
To increase muscular strength and cardiorespiratory endurance by manipulating a therapy band.

Equipment
Therapy bands or tubing

Setup
No setup required.

> ## SAFETY TIP
> Find out whether any of your students have latex allergies before selecting therapy band tubing. Tubing is available in nonlatex.

Procedure
1. Have each student begin with one or two therapy bands.
2. Have the students perform approximately 10 reps of each exercise.

    Therapy band activities:

    - Biceps curls
        - The student steps on one end of the band while holding the other end. The student pulls up on the band to perform a biceps curl.
        - Wheelchair—The student rolls one wheel on the end of the band or attaches one end of the band to the bottom of the chair.
    - Two-arm biceps curls
        - The student stands with both feet in the center of the therapy band. One hand is on each end of the band. The student lifts both hands to waist level while holding on to the therapy band and releases, repeating the sequence.
        - Wheelchair—The student rolls both wheels over the band or attaches two bands to the bottom of the chair, one on each side.
    - Flys—The student holds one end of the band in each hand with the band positioned in front of the body. The student pulls the band out and in while the arms remain straight. The student then repeats with the band overhead.
    - Rows—Wrap the band tightly around a pole or beam at the student's eye level. The student holds the band on each end and pulls back on the band in a rowing motion, repeatedly.

From left to right, the students are doing a biceps curl, an overhead fly, and a row.

Low Variations

- See the preceding wheelchair ideas.
- Attach the band to the student's wrist or hand so that the student does not have to grip the therapy band.
- When the exercise requires two hands, have the student hold one end of the band while an adult holds the other end.
- Purchase bands with the least resistance (usually labeled *light* or *easy*).

High Variations

- Use colored bands with more resistance.
- Increase the number of repetitions.
- Have students keep a journal of how many reps they do of each exercise and their improvement.
- Incorporate additional therapy band exercises.

Informal Assessment Questions

- Is the student able to hold the therapy band appropriately?
- Is the student able to manipulate the therapy band repeatedly in the specified exercises?

CHAPTER 3

Eye–Hand and Eye–Foot Coordination Activities

The 18 activities in this chapter involve coordination of the eye to hand as well as the eye to foot. These activities address tracking an object with the eye in order to contact it with the hand or foot appropriately. Skills that demonstrate eye–hand and eye–foot coordination include striking an object using an implement (e.g., bat, paddle, hockey stick), kicking a ball, and throwing a ball toward a target. When performing these types of skills toward a target, students need to demonstrate appropriate aim, force, and accuracy. In many cases, students who are unable to use their hands in an activity may use their feet. For example, a child with cerebral palsy may be able to move a foot better than a hand to propel an object. For this reason many activities in this chapter can be modified to use the hand or the foot depending on the needs of the student and the goals of the lesson.

Air Hockey Knockdown

Primary Concept
Eye–hand coordination

Secondary Concepts
Aim, force, accuracy

Activity Goal
To push a beanbag across a table surface in an attempt to knock down the "pins."

Equipment
Beanbags; water bottles (1/4 cup, or 57 g, of sand in the bottom for weight); table or flat surface

Setup
At one end of the table arrange the "pins" (water bottles) in an upright position. The student then stands or sits at the opposite end of the table facing the pin setup.

Procedure
1. Place one beanbag at a time in front of the student.
2. Cue the student to push the beanbag across the table and try to knock down the pins.

Low Variations
- Help the student push the beanbag across the table.
- Have the student use an implement to push the beanbag across the table.
- Give the student a ball or a larger object to roll across the table for a higher success rate.
- Use more pins.

High Variations
- Use fewer pins and spread them apart so that the student must demonstrate a more accurate aim.
- Have the student count the pins that have fallen and those that are still standing.
- Allow the student to set up the pins for the next player.
- Mark points on the bottles, and have students add up the points they score when knocking the pins down.

Informal Assessment Questions
- Is the student releasing the beanbag appropriately toward the pins?
- Is the student using proper aim and force, and is the push or throw accurate?

Ball Attack

Primary Concept
Eye–hand coordination

Secondary Concepts
Striking; cardiorespiratory endurance

Activity Goal
To work together to propel a large ball to a designated location by striking it with noodles.

Equipment
Large therapy ball; pool noodles cut in half; visible tape

Setup
In a large play area, use the tape (or chalk) to mark a pathway (straight, zigzag, or curved) on the ground.

Procedure
1. Have the students line up facing each other along the pathway.
2. Indicate a starting point and finishing point at each end of the pathway.
3. Place the large therapy ball at the starting point of the pathway.
4. Give each student a pool noodle half. This is what they will use to strike the ball so that it travels along the pathway to the finish line.
5. On your signal, students work together to propel the large ball between the lines on the ground by striking it with their noodles. Students must remain stationary along the pathway, and they must strike the ball as it rolls past them.

Low Variations
- Use the hand-over-hand technique (physically assist).
- If student cannot grip the noodle, use a velcro strap to secure it firmly to the arm.
- Have students work together to propel a beach ball off the end of a table.
- Replace the therapy ball with a beach ball, balloon, or extra large plastic ball.

High Variations
- Mark a large square on the ground using the visible tape. Place the therapy ball inside the square. Have the students work together to knock the therapy ball out of the square by throwing yarn balls at it.
- Have students use only yarn balls (no noodles).
- Place the therapy ball on top of a box or other raised surface. Students work together to throw yarn balls at the therapy ball to try to get it to fall off the box or surface.

Informal Assessment Questions

- Is the student holding the pool noodle appropriately for striking?
- Is the student making contact with the therapy ball by striking it?

Beach Ball Golf

Primary Concept
Eye–hand coordination

Secondary Concepts
Striking; aim, force, accuracy

Activity Goal
To demonstrate a golf swing by striking a beach ball using a pool noodle, causing the ball to reach a designated target.

Equipment
Pool noodles or paddles; beach balls; hula hoops

Setup
Organize a golf course by placing hula hoops randomly in the play area. Number the hula hoops 1 through 10 (you can use more hoops or fewer depending on the students' ability level). The hula hoops represent golf holes. Approximately 25 feet (7.6 m) from each hoop, create a line or place a cone. This is the starting point for that particular hole.

Procedure
1. Position the student at the starting point for the designated hole. (If you have multiple students, position them to start at different holes.)
2. Students propel the beach ball forward using the pool noodle or paddle and try to get the beach ball to reach the designated hoop, or "hole," using as few strikes as possible.
3. Once the student gets the beach ball into the hoop, he or she moves on to the next hole and repeats the task.
4. Count how many strikes it takes the student to reach the designated hoop.

Low Variations
- Do not count how many strikes it takes students to reach the hoop.
- Set the starting point for the hole closer.
- Use fewer holes (hoops).

High Variations
- Have students record how may strikes it take them to reach the hoop at each hole. Then, have them count the total number of strikes they had.
- Set up more holes (hoops).
- Set the starting point farther from the target.
- Make the targets smaller or more difficult to reach.
- Use a smaller ball.

Informal Assessment Questions

- Is the student striking toward the hula hoop?
- Is the student able to verbally track how many strikes it took to reach the designated hole?

Beanbag Shuffleboard

Primary Concept
Eye–hand coordination

Secondary Concepts
Aim, force, accuracy

Activity Goal
To push a beanbag forward using the hands and try to get it to land within a designated triangle pattern.

Equipment
Beanbags; table; visible tape

Setup
At one end of the table, use the tape to create a large triangle. Break the triangle into three or more sections. Designate points for each section (e.g., the top of the triangle is worth 30 points, the middle is worth 20, and the bottom is worth 10).

Procedure
1. Position the student at the opposite end of the table from the triangle design.
2. Have the student push a beanbag toward the triangle, attempting to land it within the pattern for specified points.

Low Variations
- Position the student closer to the triangle.
- Have the student use an implement to propel the beanbag forward.
- Use a small ball that will roll easily on the table, and allow the student to earn points if the ball passes through a section of the triangle, rather than having to land in it.
- Make the triangle and the sections larger.

High Variations
- Make the triangle and the sections smaller.
- Set up multiple triangles so that students have to position their bodies appropriately to propel the beanbag toward the chosen triangle.
- Position the student farther from the triangle.
- Have students add up the points they earn.

Informal Assessment Questions
- Is the student using proper aim and force and landing the beanbag accurately in the designated triangle pattern?
- Is the student releasing the beanbag appropriately toward the triangle pattern?

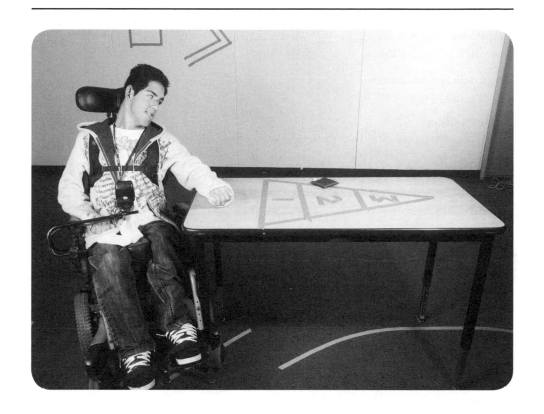

Circle Bowling

Primary Concept
Eye–hand coordination

Secondary Concepts
Rolling; aim, force, accuracy

Activity Goal
To knock down the bowling pins by rolling the ball forward.

Equipment
Bowling pins or empty plastic bottles (e.g., coffee creamer bottles, 2-liter soda bottles) (approximately 10); large ball

Setup
Position the students in a circle either sitting in chairs or on the ground. Place the bowling pins in a cluster in the center of the circle.

Procedure
1. Have one student begin with the ball and roll the ball forward in an attempt to knock down the bowling pins.
2. Have the next student attempt to knock down the remaining pins, and repeat until all the pins are down.
3. Have the higher-level students go to the center of the circle and set up the bowling pins to play again.

Low Variations
- Use a larger rolling ball.
- Have the students roll the ball off their laps or down ramps.
- Have students move closer to the bowling pins.

High Variations
- Have students stand up to roll the ball.
- Focus on form: Step with the opposite foot forward, bend knees, eyes on the target.
- Use multiple balls.
- Break the group apart and have individual bowling games.

Informal Assessment Questions
- Is the student able to release the ball toward the bowling pins?
- Is the student able to roll the ball from the appropriate distance?

Circle Soccer

Primary Concept
Eye–foot coordination

Secondary Concepts
Kicking; aim, force, accuracy

Activity Goal
To strike the ball using only the feet.

Equipment
Large ball; one chair per student

Setup
Place chairs in a circle facing the center.

Procedure
1. Have the students sit on chairs in the circle.
2. Begin by standing in the middle of the circle. Roll the ball individually to each student and have them kick it back to you. Repeat until all of the students have gotten the hang of it.
3. Now, step out of the circle and have the students try to kick the ball randomly around the circle, keeping it moving without using their hands.

Low Variations
- Allow students to use their hands to gain control of the ball before kicking.
- Allow students to kick with both feet.
- Allow students to kick using their wheelchairs (i.e., with a quick forward push).
- Place bowling pins in the middle of the circle, and have students kick toward the pins.

High Variations
- Have students kick while in a crab position (belly button pointed up, both hands and both feet on the ground).
- Have students say the name of a person in the circle and attempt to kick the ball to that person.
- Challenge students: "How many times can you kick the ball in a row?"
- Use a smaller (soccer size) ball.
- Use multiple balls.

Informal Assessment Questions
- Is the student able to make contact with the ball using the feet?
- Is the student using only the feet for the duration of the activity?

Cooperative Marble Pass

Primary Concept
Eye–hand coordination

Secondary Concept
Teamwork

Activity Goal
To get a marble from one end of a room to the other by passing it using a cardboard mailing tube. The goal is to move the marble as quickly as possible without dropping it.

Equipment
Cardboard mailing tube cut in half lengthwise (one half per student); marbles or small balls that roll easily

Setup
Find a large area free of obstacles.

Procedure
1. Have the students line up side by side at approximately the same level (if some use wheelchairs, have all student sit down, otherwise all can be standing).
2. Give each student a cardboard mailing tube (half), and have them hold it with both hands in front of their bodies so that both ends of the tubing match up with those of the students on either side of them.
3. Start the marble at one end of the student lineup. The students maneuver their tubes, causing the marble to roll to the tubes of the students next to them. The next students repeat until the marble reaches the last student in the lineup.
4. If the ball drops, the students start over from the beginning.

Low Variations
- Assist the student using a hand-over-hand technique.
- Place the mailing tube on the student's lap or on a table for extra support.

High Variations
- Time the students.
- To create a longer distance, once the students have passed the marble, have them run to the end of the line to pass it again.
- Have only two students pass the marble to each other by running to the other side once they have passed the marble. Have them cover a specified distance.

Informal Assessment Questions

- Is the student able to hold the cardboard tube appropriately?
- Is the student able to transfer the marble to another student's tube?

Foxtail Golf

Primary Concept
Eye–hand coordination

Secondary Concepts
Throwing; aim, force, accuracy

Activity Goal
To demonstrate an underhand toss by swinging the foxtail in a forward motion, causing it to reach a designated target.

Equipment
Foxtail; buckets or targets; cones

- You can make homemade foxtails using tennis balls, an old sheet, and duct tape.
  - Cut the sheet into strips approximately 3 feet (90 cm) long and 3 inches (7.5 cm) wide.
  - Tape the strip to one end of the tennis ball; then wrap duct tape around the entire tennis ball until it is covered, leaving the majority of the sheet exposed.

Setup
Set up the play area like a golf course, using designated buckets or targets as the holes. Number the targets 1 through 10 (you can use more targets or fewer depending on your students' level). Approximately 25 feet (7.5 m) from each target or bucket, create a line or place a cone. This will be the starting point for that particular hole.

Procedure
1. Have the student begin at the starting point for the designated hole. (If you have multiple students, they can each start at different holes.)
2. The object is for the students to demonstrate an underhand toss by swinging the foxtail forward and trying to reach the designated hole.
3. Count how many tosses it takes the student to reach the hole by swinging the foxtail forward.
4. Once the student has gotten the foxtail into the hole, have the student move on to the next hole and repeat the task.

Low Variations
- Do not count how many throws it takes the student to reach the hole.
- Set the starting point for the hole closer.
- Use fewer holes.
- Have the student propel the foxtail in a forward and backward motion (like a pendulum), rather than a circular motion.

High Variations

- Have the student record how many throws it takes to reach the target at each hole. Then, have the student count the total number of throws.
- Set up more holes.
- Set the starting point farther from the target.
- Make the holes smaller or more difficult to reach.

Informal Assessment Questions

- Is the student swinging the foxtail appropriately?
- Is the student swinging the foxtail toward the hole?

Hit the Can

Primary Concept
Eye–hand coordination

Secondary Concepts
Throwing; rolling; aim, force, accuracy

Activity Goal
To throw or roll a ball at a designated target from varying distances.

Equipment
Beanbags or small balls; 10 to 20 empty cans or plastic bottles of various sizes

Setup
In a large playing area, set up the cans or bottles in a horizontal line starting at a 5-foot (1.5 m) distance and increasing to 10 feet (3 m). Mark point values on the cans or bottles, putting higher numbers on the smaller objects.

Procedure
1. Position students so that they are facing the can or bottle setup.
2. Give students a beanbag to throw or roll at the cans or bottles.
3. The beanbag must make contact with the can or bottle to count for points (the can or bottle does not need to fall over).

Low Variations
- Use larger targets and a larger beanbag or ball.
- Use more targets for a higher success.
- Set cans or bottles closer.

High Variations
- Have students calculate points.
- Use fewer cans or bottles so that they are more difficult to hit.
- Have students throw from a farther distance.

Informal Assessment Questions
- Is the student able to release the beanbag by throwing or rolling it toward the cans?
- Is the student using appropriate aim and force and demonstrating accuracy?

Aluminum cans may be used as targets—some students love the sound of the crashing cans!

Knock It Out

Primary Concept
Eye–hand coordination

Secondary Concepts
Rolling; aim, force, accuracy

Activity Goal
To roll a small ball at a larger ball to knock it out of a designated area.

Equipment
Beach balls; tape for marking a designated circle; small balls that roll well; bowling ramp (if applicable)

Setup
Create a circle on the ground approximately 30 feet (9 m) in diameter. Place one beach ball in the center of the circle. Have the students sit or stand around the outside of the circle.

Procedure
1. Have the students roll the small ball at the beach ball in the center of the circle one at a time.
2. Have the students continue to take turns rolling the small ball at the beach ball until the beach ball has been knocked out of the designated circle.
3. Add beach balls to the center of the circle and have students try to knock all of the beach balls out of the circle.

Low Variations
- Use a bowling ramp to help students roll the ball.
- Use a hand-over-hand technique (physically assist).
- Have the students push the ball from their laps.
- Have students verbalize how they want to be positioned to make contact with the beach ball.

High Variations
- Have students focus on using bowling form (i.e., releasing the ball low to the ground).
- Encourage students to use strategies for knocking the ball out of the circle (line up, bend knees, etc.).
- Have higher-level students assist others.

Informal Assessment Questions
- Is the student able to contact the larger ball with the smaller ball?
- Is the student able to release the smaller ball in a rolling motion?

Here students are playing a high variation. Letting them throw instead of roll, all at the same time, provides more action while achieving the same goal of using a small ball to knock a large ball out of a designated area.

Modified Bocce Ball

Primary Concept
Eye–hand coordination

Secondary Concepts
Grasp and release; aim, force, accuracy

Activity Goal
To release a ball down a tube toward a designated target and have it stop as close to the target as possible.

Equipment
Small ball or marble; slightly larger ball or different color ball or marble (the target); hollow tube (cardboard mailing tube works well)

Setup
Find a large flat ground surface with no obstacles. Place the second marble or larger ball (target) in the center of the play area.

Procedure
1. Have the student sit in a chair at one end of the playing area.
2. Hold the cardboard tube directly in front of the student at eye level, tilted with one end slightly toward the ground.
3. Have the student verbalize how to position the tube to line it up with the target (the ball in the center of the play area).
4. Once the tube is positioned to the student's satisfaction, have the student place the marble on the tube causing it to roll toward the target.
5. The object is for the marble to reach as close to the target as possible.

Low Variations
- If the student is nonverbal, you can ask yes/no questions that the student can answer with a head nod when negotiating the position of the tube.
- Use a hand-over-hand technique to assist the student in releasing the marble down the tube.
- Ask the student whether the marble is close to or far from the target.

High Variations
- Allow the student multiple attempts to roll the marble down the tubing.
- Discuss positioning of the tubing through trial and error.
- Have the student measure the distance between the rolled marble and the target.

Informal Assessment Questions
- Is the student able to position the tube toward the target?
- Is the student able to recognize the distance between the target and the marble?

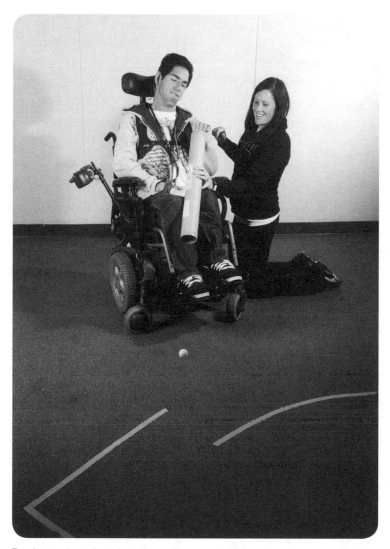

For this student, the tube is lower than eye level in order to accommodate his arm movement.

Power Chair Joust

Primary Concept
Eye–hand coordination

Secondary Concepts
Striking; moving in general space

Activity Goal
To knock a ball off a cone as quickly as possible using a pool noodle.

Equipment
Pool noodles (long); cones (at least two); medium-size balls (at least two)

Setup
In a large playing area free of obstacles, set two cones approximately 5 feet (1.5 m) apart. Place one ball on top of each cone.

Procedure
1. At least two students must participate in this activity.
2. Have one student at each end of the play area and the cones (each with a ball placed on top) in the center. Have students face each other.
3. Assign each student a ball to aim for.
4. Give each student a pool noodle.
5. On your signal, have the students move forward in their power chairs at the same time. The object is to knock the assigned ball off the designated cone using the pool noodle as quickly as possible (before the other student does the same).

Low Variations
- If the student is unable to use his or her hands, attach the pool noodle to the side of the student's chair so that the majority of the noodle is in front of the wheelchair.
- Have a peer assistant or adult push the student's wheelchair.

High Variations
- Follow the step-by-step procedure, but set up multiple cones with a ball on top of each for students to knock down as quickly as possible. Have a referee hold up a colored flag to determine the winner.
- Have multiple students participate in the activity. Set up multiple cones (with a ball on top of each) in the play area. Give each student a specific color of ball to knock down.

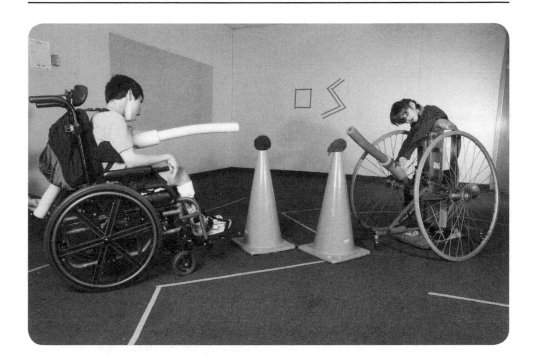

Informal Assessment Questions

- Is the student able to manipulate the pool noodle to knock the ball off the cone?
- Is the student able to move in the designated play area safely?

Three in a Row!

Primary Concept
Eye–hand coordination

Secondary Concepts
Throwing; aim, force, accuracy

Activity Goal
To throw beanbags into hoops to create a three-in-a-row pattern.

Equipment
Beanbags (approximately nine); nine hula hoops

Setup
Arrange the hula hoops in a square pattern (this is your tic-tac-toe board). First, lay down a horizontal line of three hoops, followed by a second line of three hoops directly below the first, and a third line of three hoops directly below the second. Designate a starting area approximately 5 feet (1.5 m) from the third line of hula hoops. This is where the student will be positioned.

Procedure
1. Have the student positioned on the starting line (draw a line or use a poly spot) at the bottom of the hula hoop square with a beanbag in hand.
2. The student attempts to throw the beanbag into one of the hula hoops on the tic-tac-toe board.
3. The student continues to throw beanbags one at a time until a three-in-a-row design is created (it can be vertical, horizontal, or diagonal).

Low Variations
- Use a hand-over-hand technique (physically assist).
- Create the tic-tac-toe board at a higher level (on a table).
- Create the tic-tac-toe board at a higher level and use tape in place of the hula hoops. Then have students push the beanbags into the designated squares (they can also use a hockey puck).
- Use a larger, lighter, or easier-to-grasp object for throwing.

High Variations
- Have students throw from farther away.
- Use smaller hula hoops.
- Play other forms of the tic-tac-toe game.
  - Four corners
  - Blackout
- Call out the type of line you would like the student to create (vertical, horizontal, diagonal).
- Have students play against one another.

Informal Assessment Questions

- Is the student able to release the beanbag toward the tic-tac-toe board?
- Is the student able to recognize a three-in-a-row design?

Throw It; Then Roll It!

Primary Concept
Eye–hand coordination

Secondary Concepts
Throwing; rolling; aim, force, accuracy

Activity Goal
To demonstrate cooperation by throwing a beanbag into open space, and then rolling a ball and trying to have it to land as close to the beanbag as possible.

Equipment
Yarn balls (one per student); beanbags (one for every two students)

Setup
Find a large playing area with a flat surface and no obstacles.

Procedure
1. Have the students get into pairs (choose an appropriate way to partner students).
2. Give each student one yarn ball and each pair of students one beanbag.
3. One student begins by throwing the beanbag wherever desired in the play area (short throw or long throw).
4. Students then take turns rolling their yarn balls to try to get them as close to the beanbag as possible.
5. Whoever is closer to the beanbag gets to start the next round by throwing the beanbag where desired.
6. If students disagree about which ball is closer, have them measure the distance from their balls to the beanbag by using their feet.

Low Variations
- Allow students to push from their laps or drop their balls toward the beanbag.
- Have students play as a group, sitting in a large circle. Each student rolls a yarn ball, trying to get it as close as possible to the beanbag in the center of the circle.
- Allow students to use ramps or cardboard mailing tubes to roll the ball.

High Variations
- This is a great activity to use with pedometers!
- Discuss aim, force, and accuracy.
- Use a ruler to determine which ball is closer to the beanbag.

Informal Assessment Questions

- Does the student take turns appropriately?
- Is the student able to identify which ball is closer to the beanbag?

Spray Down

Primary Concept
Eye–hand coordination

Secondary Concepts
Grasp and release; aim, force, accuracy

Activity Goal
To cause a Ping-Pong ball to fall off a water bottle or cone by spraying it with water from a spray bottle.

Equipment
Spray bottle; Ping-Pong ball; water bottle or cone

Setup
Fill the spray bottle with water. Set the Ping-Pong ball on top of the water bottle or cone, and place it on a table or at eye level.

> ### SAFETY TIP
> Place towels under the bottles to soak up the water, or play the activity on a grassy area to avoid wet floors.

Procedure
1. Position the student approximately 3 feet (1 m) from the Ping-Pong ball with the spray bottle in hand.
2. On your signal, have the student spray water at the Ping-Pong ball in an attempt to knock it off the water bottle or cone.
3. Set up multiple Ping-Pong balls for multiple attempts or multiple players.

Low Variations
- Position the student closer to the target.
- Adjust the spray bottle to be a more direct water stream rather than a spray.
- Allow the student to use the hands or another body part or to use an implement to knock the Ping-Pong ball off.

High Variations
- Set up multiple Ping-Pong balls on cones or water bottles and see how fast the student can knock them all down.
- Have students race one another.

Informal Assessment Questions
- Is the student able to knock the Ping-Pong ball off the water bottle?
- Is the student able to manipulate the water bottle appropriately to spray the water in a constant motion?

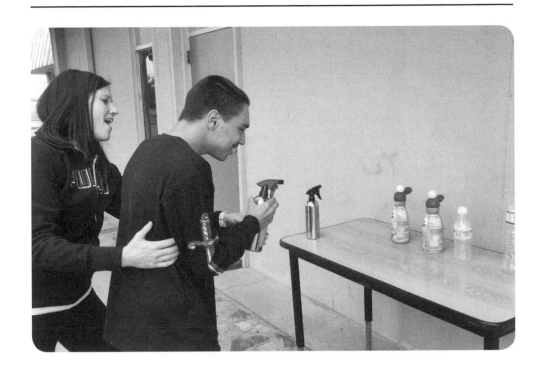

String Ball

Primary Concept
Eye–hand coordination

Secondary Concept
Crossing the midline

Activity Goal
To push a ball from one side of the body to the other using one hand to cross the midline, while passing the ball to another student.

Equipment
Wiffle ball; string

Setup
Run the string through the Wiffle ball (like threading a bead). Tie the ends of the string to two stationary points such as a door knob and chair. Position student so that the ball is in front of the body within arm's reach.

Procedure
1. Position the student so that the ball is in front of the body at eye level, within arm's reach.
2. Have the student hold the ball with the dominant hand and move it so that it crosses the midline of the body (right to left or left to right).

Low Variations
- Demonstrate using a hand-over-hand technique (i.e., physically assist) until the student grasps the concept.
- Have the student visually track the ball while another student moves it.

High Variations
- Have the students sit in a circle and hold the string. Students slide the ball along the string to the person next to them until the ball makes a complete circle.
- Have students play a game similar to hot potato. When the music stops, the person who is touching the ball must do something. For example, clap their hands a number of times, sing a song, turn around in their space, or whatever is a good match their skill level.
- Add multiple Wiffle balls.

Informal Assessment Questions
- Is the student able to move the ball by crossing the midline?
- Is the student able to anticipate which side the ball is coming from?

Swing Bowling

Primary Concept
Eye–hand coordination

Secondary Concepts
Aim, force, accuracy

Activity Goal
To push a ball suspended by a rope into standing bowling pins to knock them down.

Equipment
Rope approximately 20 feet (6 m) long (or a Soccer Pal); playground-size ball; pillowcase; bowling pins or lightweight containers that can be knocked over easily (e.g., quart or liter milk containers or water bottles); suspended hook or basketball rim

Setup
Place a ball in a pillowcase and then tie a rope around the closed pillowcase. Attach the other end of the rope to a suspended hook or basketball rim so that the ball hangs about 1 foot (30 cm) from the ground. Directly behind the ball, set up the bowling pins in a cluster on the ground. Position the student approximately 10 feet (3 m) away, facing the ball.

Procedure
1. Have the student face the bowling pins at a 10-foot (3 m) distance.
2. Have the student hold the ball with both hands or on the lap.
3. On the cue "Go," the student releases the ball in a forward motion to try to knock down the bowling pins.

Low Variations
- Assist the student using a hand-over-hand technique.
- Use a lighter or larger ball.
- Set up more pins.

High Variations
- Have the student positioned at different angles from the bowling pins.
- Spread the pins out so that the student has to aim the ball.

Informal Assessment Questions
- Is the student able to release the ball in a forward direction toward the bowling pins?
- Is the student able to get into an appropriate position to knock down as many pins as possible?

CHAPTER 4

Moving in General Space Activities

The 12 activities in this chapter address moving within specified boundaries safely, without bumping into others. Many activities that involve moving in general space allow a student to move around freely while following specific movement cues or prepositions (e.g., *stop, go, under, around, up*). Other skills recognized within this category include chasing, fleeing, and dodging. These movement skills are often seen in cooperative tag games, in which a person must either tag or avoid being tagged by another player.

Bubble Wrap Stomp

Primary Concept
Moving in general space

Secondary Concepts
Creative movement; rhythm and beat

Activity Goal
To pop the bubble wrap by stomping on it or using a designated body part while following the beat of a song.

Equipment
Bubble wrap (large bubbles work best) (approximately 15 ft, or 4.5 m); music or a drum (something that distinguishes a beat)

Setup
Lay out bubble wrap in a large play area free of obstacles.

Procedure
1. Have students stand at the edge of the bubble wrap (with or without shoes on).
2. Explain what it means to move to the beat of the music or a drum.
3. On your signal, have the students stomp on the bubble wrap to the beat of the music or drum.
4. Now challenge students to use a different body part to pop the bubble wrap.

Low Variations
- Allow students to roll over the bubble wrap with wheelchairs, walkers, or crutches.
- Place the bubble wrap on a table in front of the students and allow them to use their hands to pop the bubbles.
- Focus on students' successfully popping the bubbles and not on moving to the beat of the music or drum.

High Variations
- Speed up the rhythm so that students are required to move more quickly.
- Put together a pattern (e.g., stomp with the right foot, the left foot, the right hand, and then the left hand).

Informal Assessment Questions
- Is the student able to pop the bubbles on the bubble wrap using a designated body part?
- Is the student able to pop the bubbles to the beat of the music or drum?

Crazy Cones

Primary Concept
Moving in general space

Secondary Concepts
Chasing, fleeing, dodging; movement pathways

Activity Goal
To knock down or set up cones in a timely manner.

Equipment
Cones (approximately 20); pool noodles cut in half

Setup
Set up the cones randomly throughout the play area. Cut pool noodles in half.

Procedure
1. Have the students line up on one side of the play area (use poly spots to designate a location if necessary). Give each student a pool noodle half.
2. On your signal, the students run and knock down all of the cones in the play area using their noodles.
3. When all the cones are down, the students run back to their poly spots or designated locations. This completes the round.
4. Now, on your signal, the students set the cones back up. When all the cones are set up and students are back on their poly spots, the round is complete.
5. Time the students, and repeat the activity to see if they can beat their time.

Low Variations
- Use larger cones or set cones on boxes or crates so that they are at a higher level.
- Use fewer cones.

High Variations
- Use more cones.
- Split the class in half and set poly spots on both ends of the playing area. Scatter the cones in the playing area randomly, half knocked down, half standing up. Have one team knock down the cones and the other team set the cones back up. Give students approximately five minutes to play. Then, on your signal, have the students go back to their poly spots. Higher-level students on each team can count how many cones are standing and how many are down.

Informal Assessment Questions

- Is the student knocking down or setting up the cones as specified?
- Is the student moving in general space appropriately without running into others?

Fill the Basket

Primary Concept
Moving in general space

Secondary Concept
Grasp and release

Activity Goal
To move in general space while gathering objects to place in a designated location.

Equipment
Yarn balls or lightweight objects easy to grasp (approximately 20); large cones, milk crates, or cardboard boxes (anything that can bring an object closer to eye level); two hula hoops

Setup
In a large play area arrange the cones randomly. Place at least one yarn ball on each cone. Place one hula hoop at each end of the play area.

Procedure
1. On your signal, have the students maneuver through the play area and pick up a yarn ball.
2. The students then carry the yarn ball to one of the hula hoops and place it there before returning to the play area to retrieve another yarn ball.
3. The students must pick up the yarn balls one at a time.
4. The activity is complete when all of the yarn balls are in the hoops.

Low Variations
- Student may place the yarn balls on their laps to carry them to the hula hoops.
- Use larger objects or objects that are easier to grasp.
- Use Velcro balls, and have students use Velcro mitts to pick them up.

High Variations
- Break the class up into two teams, and have each team retrieve specific colored objects to take to its team hula hoop. See which team can retrieve all its objects the quickest.
- Set the yarn balls on the ground.
- Have students maneuver through the play area on scooter boards.

Informal Assessment Questions
- Is the student moving in general space without running into others?
- Is the student placing the yarn balls in the hula hoops?

Here a variety of objects are being used to make the task more interesting.

Follow the Leader Obstacle Course

Primary Concept
Moving in general space

Secondary Concepts
Movement pathways; prepositional concepts

Activity Goal
To demonstrate movement through an obstacle course while acting as the leader or the follower.

Equipment
Tape (if inside); sidewalk chalk (if outside); approximately 10 cones, poly spots, or other obstacles that students can maneuver under, over, around, through, and so on

Setup
In a large play area, mark lines on the ground with tape (inside) or chalk (outside) to designate pathways. Or, if you are using a gym, use the lines that mark the basketball court area. If you are on a playground, use the playground markings. Set up cones in a straight line approximately 2 feet (61 cm) apart. Arrange the poly spots randomly in the play area.

Procedure
1. Arrange the students in pairs. Designate one student as the leader and the other as the follower.
2. Allow the students to use the entire play area to play follow the leader.
3. Demonstrate to students the kinds of movements they can do within the obstacle course:
   - Walk straight with both feet on the line, one foot on the line and one foot off, or straddling a straight line on the ground. (Students in wheelchairs can roll with their right or left wheel on the line or can straddle the line with their wheels.)
   - Weave between cones.
   - Circle around poly spots; jump over poly spots. (For students in wheelchairs, one big push can represent a jump.)
4. Allow leaders to be creative. After about six minutes, switch students so that the leader is now the follower and the follower is now the leader.

Low Variations
- Have the class play as a group with everyone following one leader.
- Have student verbalize where they would like to move while you maneuver them through the play area.
- Use more visual stimuli within the course, such as things hanging, cause-and-effect activities (such as switch toys), and so on.

High Variations

- Have students vary their speed within the obstacle course based on your commands.
- Have students maneuver through the course on scooter boards.
- Create more obstacles (e.g., tunnels, hurdles, hoops).

Informal Assessment Questions

- Is the student able to move through the play area safely without bumping into others?
- Is the follower able to mirror the leader's movements?

Noodle Tag

Primary Concept
Moving in general space

Secondary Concepts
Chasing, fleeing, dodging; cardiorespiratory endurance

Activity Goal
To demonstrate cooperative tag while manipulating a noodle.

Equipment
Two pool noodles cut in half

Setup
Find a large, flat play area free of obstacles. Cut pool noodles in half.

SAFETY TIP
Remind students of appropriate ways to tag their peers. Guidelines may include tagging only below the waist and using a gentle tag.

Procedure
1. Have the students spread out in the play area.
2. Designate four students (depending on class size) to be taggers.
3. The remaining students are the dodgers who try to avoid the taggers.
4. Give each tagger a noodle with which to tag the dodgers.
5. On your signal, the students move around in the play area.
6. Students who are tagged must freeze where they are and remain still until another tagger touches them with a noodle to unfreeze them.
7. After approximately five minutes, designate new taggers.

Low Variations
- Help taggers maneuver through the play area so that they can focus on holding the noodle to tag.
- Students can play the role of both tagger and dodger by tagging other students while also avoiding being tagged.

High Variations
- Have students play on scooter boards.
- Have students use a variety of locomotor skills while maneuvering through the play area (e.g., skip, gallop, slide, walk, jump).

Informal Assessment Questions

- Is the student able to move in general space safely?
- Is the student freezing in place when tagged with a noodle?

Rhythm Sticks and Musical Instruments

Primary Concept
Moving in general space

Secondary Concepts
Creative movement; rhythm and beat; prepositional concepts

Activity Goal
To manipulate rhythm sticks or a musical instrument to the rhythm or beat of the music.

Equipment
Rhythm sticks (two per student); musical instruments (e.g., drums, maracas, bells, tambourines—one per student); appropriate music and music player

- Kimbo Educational: *Ball, Hoop & Ribbon Activities for Young Children* CD
- Greg & Steve: *Kids in Action* CD
- The Learning Station: *Rock 'N' Roll Songs That Teach* CD and *Sift and Splash* CD

Setup
No setup required.

Procedure
1. Have the students manipulate their musical instruments or tap their rhythm sticks to the beat of the music by mirroring your movements while also moving in general space.
2. Cue the students to manipulate their instruments or sticks to the left, right, high, low, behind, and in front.
3. Cue the students to manipulate their instruments or sticks at a fast, medium, or slow pace.
4. Have the students start and stop on cue.

Low Variations
- Use a hand-over-hand technique (physically assist).
- Have the student hold one stick while you tap on it with the other stick.
- Use a Velcro strap to attach the instrument to the student's wrist so that the student doesn't have to grasp the instrument.
- Place the instrument on a table in front of the student or on the student's lap (e.g., a drum).
- Have the student manipulate the instrument or sticks in a stationary position.

High Variations

- Have a student pass out the rhythm sticks or instruments to the class.
- Have higher-level students assist lower-level students (hand over hand).
- Have students identify their instruments by name.
- Encourage students to sing the words to the song.
- Have students create a dance or movement sequence using the sticks or instruments.
- Create a marching band by having students line up and move around the room playing their instruments.

Informal Assessment Questions

- Is the student able to manipulate the instrument or rhythm sticks to the appropriate beat?
- Is the student moving in space safely, without bumping into others?

Scarves and Ribbon Sticks

Primary Concept
Moving in general space

Secondary Concepts
Creative movement; rhythm and beat

Activity Goal
To manipulate a scarf or ribbon stick while moving to the rhythm or beat of the music.

Equipment
Scarves or ribbons sticks (one or two per student); movement music and music player

- To make homemade ribbon sticks, attach ribbons or streamers to a ring or a dowel.
- Kimbo Educational: *Ball, Hoop & Ribbon Activities for Young Children* CD
- Greg & Steve: *Kids in Action* CD
- The Learning Station: *Rock 'N' Roll Songs That Teach* CD and *Sift and Splash* CD

Setup
Find a large play area free of obstacles.

Procedure
1. Have the students begin with one scarf or ribbon stick (two if students are more advanced).
2. Have the students mirror various ways to move the scarf or ribbon stick:
   - Big circles
   - Up high, down low
   - To the left, to the right
   - In front of or behind the body
   - Fast or slow
   - Throw up and catch (scarf)
   - Throw up, clap, and catch (scarf)
   - Throw up, spin in a circle, and catch (scarf)
3. Play music and have the students move their scarves or ribbon sticks to the beat.
4. Allow the students to be creative in moving their scarves or ribbon sticks to the music.

Low Variations

- Use a hand-over-hand technique (physically assist).
- Tie the scarf or ribbon to a bracelet and place it around the student's wrist.
- Have the student manipulate the scarf or ribbon while standing or sitting still.

High Variations

- Have the student pass out the scarves or ribbon sticks to classmates.
- Have a student lead the movements and have the rest of the class copy him or her.
- Have the students make up two-, three-, or four-part routines.

Informal Assessment Questions

- Is the student able to manipulate the scarf or ribbon stick to the beat?
- Is the student moving in space safely, without bumping into others?

Steal the Chicken

Primary Concept
Moving in general space

Secondary Concepts
Chasing, fleeing, dodging; cardiorespiratory endurance

Activity Goal
To maneuver through space to retrieve an object before one's partner, and then return to one's designated spot without getting tagged.

Equipment
Rubber chicken or small, light object that students can grasp; poly spots

Setup
Designate two spots approximately 20 feet (6 m) apart. In the center of the spots place the chicken. If the student is in a wheelchair or unable to bend over to pick up the chicken, place it on a table, a laundry basket turned upside down, or a large cone to raise it to a reaching level.

> ## SAFETY TIP
> Remind students of appropriate ways to tag their peers. Guidelines may include tagging only below the waist and using a gentle tag.

Procedure
1. Have students face each other at their respective spots.
2. On your signal, the students run to the chicken on the other student's spot as quickly as possible. The first student to reach the chicken picks it up and runs back to his or her own spot as quickly as possible.
3. The student who does not retrieve the chicken first tries to tag the opponent who has the chicken before he or she reaches the designated spot. If the student is tagged by his or her opponent before reaching the designated spot, they repeat the activity.

Low Variations
- Place the chicken at eye level (on a table or other surface).
- Rather than having the student pick up the chicken, have the student touch it, touch a button that lights up, flip over a card, or perform another similar action.
- Assist students during the activity until they understand the concept.
- Designate the grabber and tagger before the go signal. Have the tagger use a pool noodle to touch the student who has the chicken. This will give them a greater advantage of tagging by giving them a longer reach.
- Have the students play individually and time them using a stopwatch. Encourage them to try to beat their time.

High Variations

- Have students use different locomotor skills when moving toward the chicken (e.g., crab walk, bear crawl, gallop, hop).
- Designate one student as the starter. That student performs a hand gesture or posture (e.g., both hands above the head, one hand touching an ear). The other student must mirror the gesture or posture. Once both students are performing the gesture or posture, they can begin the activity (i.e., run to the chicken).

Informal Assessment Questions

- Is the student able to move in the appropriate direction both when heading out to retrieve the chicken and when trying to tag the student who has the chicken?
- Is the student able to pick up the chicken and carry it appropriately?

Stop and Go!

Primary Concept
Moving in general space

Secondary Concepts
Cardiorespiratory endurance; prepositional concepts

Activity Goal
To understand the concepts of stop and go while moving in general space.

Equipment
Stop and go signal (red/green sign, music, or instrument)

Setup
Find an empty space with designated boundaries and no obstacles.

Procedure
1. Have the students find personal space so that they are standing without touching anyone else.
2. On your cue, students move in general space without bumping into others when they see a green sign and stop when they see a red sign. If you are using music, they move when they hear the music and stop when the music stops.
3. The students do not have to move in a straight line as in the traditional game of red light, green light. Allow them to move anywhere in the designated space.

Low Variations
- If you are maneuvering a student, have the student determine when to stop and go (e.g., raise a red card for stop and a green card for go, press a button once for stop and twice for go, verbalize "stop" and "go").
- Rather than moving their bodies, allow students to move a body part, such as their hands or head, while following the stop and go signals.

High Variations
- Have the students move in general space on scooter boards.
- Have the students manipulate an object (e.g., bounce a ball, throw and catch a beanbag) while following the stop and go signals.
- Place obstacles within the boundaries.

Informal Assessment Questions
- Does the student demonstrate the appropriate motion on the stop and go signal?
- Is the student able to move in general space safely without bumping into others?

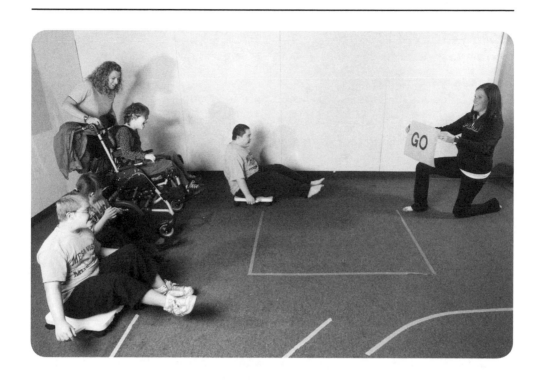

Tail Tag

Primary Concept
Moving in general space

Secondary Concepts
Chasing, fleeing, dodging; cardiorespiratory endurance

Activity Goal
To pull the tail from another student while moving in general space.

Equipment
Long knee socks, ribbon, or string (one per student)

Setup
Find a large play area free of obstacles.

Procedure
1. Have the students tuck their "tails" into their pants, leaving the majority of the tails exposed. Students in wheelchairs should tuck their tails behind their wheelchairs.
2. Have the students move in general space, attempting to grab the tail of another student.
3. Once a student has pulled a tail from another student, he or she hands the tail back to the student, who then tucks the tail back into his or her pants, and play continues.

Low Variations
- Give tails to only one or two students and have the rest try to pull the tails of the designated students.
- Help students move about the play area.
- Help students tuck in their tails.

High Variations
- Have the students move using a variety of locomotor movements.
- Have the students use dodging skills such as pivoting, spinning, and changing direction quickly to avoid having their tails taken.

Informal Assessment Questions
- Is the student able to move in the play area safely without bumping into others?
- Is the student able to pull the tail of another student appropriately?

Team Basketball

Primary Concept
Moving in general space

Secondary Concepts
Passing; teamwork; cardiorespiratory endurance

Activity Goal
To pass a ball among all team members before dropping it into a designated location for a point.

Equipment
Basketball or playground ball; two hula hoops or baskets; cones to designate boundaries (if necessary)

Setup
Find a large play area free of obstacles similar to a basketball court. Dimensions can vary based on the skills and needs of the students. Place one hula hoop or basket at each end of the play area.

Procedure
1. Divide the students into two teams.
2. Explain to the students what basket they are trying to score on.
3. The students must pass the ball among all of the players on their team before they can drop the ball into the basket for a point.
4. If the ball is taken by the opposite team and then retrieved again, that team must start the passing sequence over again.

Low Variations
- Have all participants work together as one team to score a point.
- Use a balloon or a lighter ball.
- Use a smaller ball for better grip.
- Allow students to push the ball onto the lap of a teammate.
- Allow a ball that touches a teammate to count as a pass.
- Make the play area smaller.

High Variations
- Place the basket at a higher level.
- Use more traditional basketball rules.
- Require that students say the name of the person they are passing to.

Informal Assessment Questions
- Is the student able to pass the ball to another person on his or her team?
- Is the student able to place the ball in the basket at the appropriate time?

In this variation, students must pass the ball around before shooting.

Traffic

Primary Concept
Moving in general space

Secondary Concepts
Cardiorespiratory endurance; movement concepts

Activity Goal
To move in general space while following cues for fast, medium, slow, and stop.

Equipment
Large visual signs for fast, medium, slow, and stop, or music or an instrument (drum) with a fast, medium, and slow beat

Setup
Find a large play area free of obstacles.

Procedure
1. Ensure that the students understand the concepts of fast, medium, slow, and stop.
2. Explain the signal that represents each concept, or how the rhythm of the music represents each concept.
3. On your signal, have the students move in general space without bumping into one another following your cues (fast, medium, slow, stop).

Low Variations
- Use only verbal and visual cues.
- Use only stop and go cues.

High Variations
- Use more traffic cues.
- Have students call the cues.
- Have students move on scooter boards.
- Have students move in space using specified locomotor movements (e.g., jump, gallop, skip).

Informal Assessment Questions
- Is the student able to move in general space safely without bumping into others?
- Is the student able to demonstrate the concepts of fast, medium, slow, and stop appropriately?

APPENDIX

Evidence-Based Research

Physical Activities for Young People With Severe Disabilities is based on over 30 years of experience in teaching and working with individuals with severe disabilities as well as a detailed review of the evidence-based research. Physical activity is important for the general population, including those with disabling conditions. Through regular physical activity, people with disabilities can enhance their quality of life by improving their ability to perform activities associated with daily living (Campbell & Jones, 1994; Damiano & Abel, 1998; Damiano, Vaughan, & Abel, 1995; Dodd, Taylor, & Graham, 2003; McBurney et al., 2003; Schlough et al., 2005). Legislation such as the Individuals with Disabilities Education Improvement Act (United States Congress, 2004) and government organizations such as the United States Department of Health and Human Services (USDHHS, 2000), the World Health Organization (WHO, 2010), and the Centers for Disease Control and Prevention (CDC, 2010) guide both policy and practice to increase fitness levels in people with disabilities.

Exercise intervention programs are an effective way to assess and improve the four main components of overall health for people with disabilities: muscular strength, cardiorespiratory endurance, flexibility, and psychological well-being (Damiano, Vaughan, & Abel, 1995; Dodd, Taylor, & Graham, 2003; McBurney et al., 2003; Schlough et al., 2005). Research has focused on both long-term (as long as 25 weeks) and short-term (less than 1 week) exercise programs for people with disabilities (Damiano, Vaughan, & Abel, 1995; Dodd, Taylor, & Graham, 2003; McBurney et al., 2003; Schlough et al., 2005). In fact, McBurney and colleagues (2003) found significant increases in muscular strength of the lower extremities among the participants in a 6-week exercise program designed to measure muscular strength in adolescents with cerebral palsy. These findings are consistent with other exercise intervention programs that also support the benefits of a strength-training program for children with cerebral palsy (Damiano & Abel, 1998; Dodd, Taylor, & Graham, 2003).

> Around 10% of the world's population, or 650 million people, live with disabilities (WHO, 2010).

Improving cardiorespiratory endurance allows people with disabilities to more easily keep up with the demands associated with daily living (Damiano, Vaughan, & Abel, 1995; Santiago, Coyle, & Kinney, 1993; Schlough et al., 2005; Shinohara et al., 2002). Shinohara and colleagues' 2002 study demonstrated that exercises using the lower extremities improve endurance for children with cerebral palsy.

Children and adolescents should do 60 minutes (1 hour) or more of physical activity each day (CDC, 2010).

Flexibility can enhance one's independence by easing the processes of bathing, dressing, doing housework, and performing various other tasks of daily living. Exercise intervention programs that incorporate flexibility training result in significant improvement in range of motion among people with severe physical disabilities, who tend to have both contractures and spasticity across the joints and muscles (Fragala, Goodgold, & Dumas, 2003; McPherson et al., 1984; Richards, Malouin, & Dumas, 1991; Tremblay et al., 1990). These conditions affect overall movement and can limit range of motion. When looking at treatment options, both invasive (casting and surgery) and noninvasive procedures can be implemented. Passive muscle stretching and physical exercise are noninvasive techniques that can reduce muscle spasticity and contractures, which will then allow for an increase in range of motion. In the study by Tremblay and colleagues (1990), significant changes were found in the spasticity of particular muscles that underwent prolonged muscle stretching. This study measured short-term changes of 12 children with cerebral palsy assigned to an experimental group and found that prolonged muscle stretching does reduce spasticity and demonstrates an increase in the range of motion of children with cerebral palsy.

Not only does physical activity improve overall fitness levels for independence and functioning, but it also yields positive psychological benefits for individuals with severe physical disabilities (Blinde & McClung, 1997; Campbell & Jones, 1994; Giacobbi et al., 2006). Such benefits include increased energy, a sense of personal happiness, confidence, personal responsibility, greater self-perception, increased self-esteem, and greater willingness to interact with the general population.

In 2007 (CDC), 65% of young people in grades 9 to 12 did not get the recommended amount of physical activity; 35% watched television for 3 or more hours on the average school day.

The combined physiological and psychological benefits of exercise are very encouraging for individuals' quality of life (Schlough et al., 2005). Increasing the time dedicated to exercise may enhance daily functioning and personal and social well-being for those with physical disabilities (Seaman, Corbin, & Pangrazi, 1999). Finally, programs are most effective when carried out on a regular basis with minimal breaks in intervention (Dodd, Taylor, & Graham, 2003; McBurney et al., 2003; Schlough et al., 2005; Shinohara et al., 2002).

RESOURCES ─────────────────○

In this section of the book you will find additional resources that may be helpful when working with individuals with a disability and when carrying out the activities in this book. Web sites, books, and other materials are included in this section to provide further information to support instructional activities as well as working with individuals with disabilities in a physical activity setting.

Web Sites

American Alliance for Health, Physical Education, Recreation and Dance (AAHPERD)
www.aahperd.org
This the largest national organization of professionals who both support and assist people involved in health promotion, physical education, leisure, fitness, and dance.

Human Kinetics
www.HumanKinetics.com
This is one of the largest publishers of physical activity texts and reference books for both general and adapted physical education.

National Association for Sport and Physical Education (NASPE)
www.aahperd.org/naspe
This nonprofit association sets standards for practice in sport and physical education in grades K through 12. It is one of the five national associations that make up the American Alliance for Health, Physical Education, Recreation and Dance, known as AAHPERD.

National Dissemination Center for Children with Disabilities (NICHCY)
www.nichcy.org
This Web site is a resource for educators, families, journalists, and students. It provides information on children and adolescents from birth through age 22. Topics include disability information, early intervention services, special education services, research on effective educational practices, information on the individualized education program process, disability organizations, educational rights and laws, professional associations, and transition to adult life.

PE Central
www.pecentral.org
This Web site is an online resource for teachers and educators in health and physical education in grades K through 12. It provides the most current information on lesson ideas, assessments, classroom management strategies, jobs in the field, equipment, and best practices in physical education.

Music

Greg & Steve

www.gregandsteve.com
Greg & Steve are a duo who specialize in music for children ages 3 to 9. The music of Greg & Steve is interactive and helps teach basic concepts to target learning within this age group. Below is a list of CDs recorded by Greg & Steve. These albums focus on movement and exercise.

Shake, Rattle & Rock

Ready…Set…MOVE!

Fun and Games

Kids in Motion

Kids in Action

The Learning Station

http://store.learningstationmusic.com
The Learning Station is a group of recording artists who specialize in early childhood development and education. The Learning Station has produced hundreds of interactive songs designed to enhance learning for children across the nation. Below is a list of CDs recorded by the Learning Station. These albums focus on movement and exercise.

Sift and Splash

Seasonal Songs in Motion

Brain Boogie Boosters

Rock 'n' Roll Songs That Teach

Physical Ed

Get Funky

You Can Dance

Tony Chestnut

Adapted Equipment

FlagHouse

www.flaghouse.com
FlagHouse is a supplier of equipment and resources for physical education, sports, fitness, and recreation and for health, special needs, special education, sensory integration, and multisensory environments.

School Specialty: Abilitations

www.abilitations.com
This organization focuses on movement, positioning, sensorimotor activities, education, communication, exercise, and play.

S&S

http://pe.ssww.com
S&S is a discount physical education superstore.

Gopher

www.gophersport.com
Gopher offers top-quality equipment for physical education, athletics, fitness, recreation, and health professionals.

Textbooks

Auxter, D., Pyfer, J., Zittell, L., Roth, K., & Huettig, C. (2010). *Principles and methods of adapted physical education and recreation.* New York: McGraw-Hill.

Graham, G., Holt/Hale, S.A., & Parker, M. (2007). *Children moving: A reflective approach to teaching physical education* (7th ed.). New York: McGraw-Hill.

Kasser, S.L., & Lytle, R.K. (2005). *Inclusive physical activity: A lifetime of opportunities.* Champaign, IL: Human Kinetics.

Lieberman, L., & Houston-Wilson, C. (2009). *Strategies for inclusion: A handbook for physical educators.* Champaign, IL: Human Kinetics.

Sherrill, C. (2004). *Adapted physical activity, recreation and sport: Crossdisciplinary and lifespan* (6th ed.). New York: McGraw-Hill.

Winnick, J. (2005). *Adapted physical education and sport* (4th ed.). Champaign, IL: Human Kinetics.

REFERENCES

Blinde, E.M., & McClung, L.R. (1997). Enhancing the physical and social self through recreational activity: Accounts of individuals with physical disabilities. *Adapted Physical Activity Quarterly,* 14, 327-344.

Brown, L., Branston, M.B., Hamre-Nietupski, S., Pumpian, I., Certo, N., & Gruenewald, L. (2001). A strategy for developing chronological-age-appropriate and functional curricular content for severely handicapped adolescents and young adults. *The Journal of Special Education,* 13 (1), 82-90.

Campbell, E., & Jones, G. (1994). Psychological well-being in wheelchair sport participants and nonparticipants. *Adapted Physical Activity Quarterly,* 11, 404-415.

Centers for Disease Control and Prevention (CDC). (2010). *Physical activity guidelines.* www.cdc.gov/physicalactivity/everyone/guidelines/adults.html.

Centers for Disease Control and Prevention (CDC). (2007). *Preventing chronic diseases: Investing wisely in health.* www.cdc.gov/nccdphp/publications/factsheets/Prevention/pdf/obesity.pdf.

Damiano, D.L., & Abel, M.F. (1998). Functional outcomes of strength training in spastic cerebral palsy. *Archives of Physical and Medical Rehabilitation,* 79, 119-125.

Damiano, D.L., Vaughan, C.L., & Abel, M.F. (1995). Muscle response to heavy resistance exercise in children with spastic cerebral palsy. *Developmental Medicine & Child Neurology,* 37, 731-739.

DePauw, K.P. (1996). Students with disabilities in physical education. In S.J. Silverman & C.D. Ennis (Eds.), *Student learning in physical education: Applying research to enhance instruction* (pp. 101-124). Champaign, IL: Human Kinetics.

Dodd, K.J., Taylor, N.F., & Graham, K.H. (2003). A randomized clinical trial of strength training in young people with cerebral palsy. *Developmental Medicine & Child Neurology,* 45, 652-657.

Fragala, M.A., Goodgold, S., & Dumas, H.M. (2003). Effects of lower extremity passive stretching: Pilot study of children and youth with severe limitations in self-mobility. *Pediatric Physical Therapy,* 15 (3), 167-175.

Giacobbi, P.R. Jr., Hardin, B., Frye, N., Hausenblas, H.A., Sears, S., & Stegelin, A. (2006). A multi-level examination of personality, exercise, and daily life events for individuals with physical disabilities. *Adapted Physical Activity Quarterly,* 23, 129-147.

Kasser, S.L., & Lytle, R.K. (2005). *Inclusive physical activity: A lifetime of opportunities.* Champaign, IL: Human Kinetics.

Kauffman, J.M., & Krouse, J. (1981). The cult of educability: Searching for the substance of things hoped for; the evidence of things not seen. *Analysis and Intervention in Developmental Disabilities,* 1, 53-60.

Kleinert, H.L., & Kearns, J.F. (1999). A validation study of the performance indicators and learner outcomes of Kentucky's alternative assessment for students with significant disabilities. *Journal of the Association for Persons with Severe Handicaps,* 24 (2), 100-110.

McBurney, H., Taylor, N.F., Dodd, K.J., & Graham, K.H. (2003). A qualitative analysis of the benefits of strength training for young people with cerebral palsy. *Developmental Medicine & Child Neurology,* 45, 658-663.

McPherson, J.J., Arends, T.G., Michaels, M.J., & Trettin, K. (1984). The range of motion of long knee contractures of four spastic cerebral palsied children: A pilot study. *Physical & Occupational Therapy in Pediatrics,* 4 (1), 17-34.

Meyer, L.H., Eichinger, J., & Park-Lee, S. (1987). A validation of program quality indicators in educational services for students with severe disabilities. *Journal of the Association for Persons with Severe Handicaps,* 12 (4), 251-263.

National Association for Sport and Physical Education (NASPE). (2004). *Moving into the future: National standards for physical education* (2nd ed.). Reston, VA: McGraw-Hill.

Richards, C.L., Malouin, F., & Dumas, F. (1991). Effects of a single session of prolonged planter flexor stretch on muscle activations during gait in spastic cerebral palsy. *Scandinavian Journal of Rehabilitation Medicine,* 23, 103-111.

Santiago, M.C., Coyle, C.P., & Kinney, W.B. (1993). Aerobic exercise effects on individuals with physical disabilities. *Archives of Physical Medicine and Rehabilitation,* 74, 1192-1197.

Schlough, K., Nawoczenski, D., Case, L.E, Nolan, K., & Wiggleworth, J.K. (2005). The effects of aerobic exercise on endurance, strength, function, and self-perception in adolescents with spastic cerebral palsy: A report of three case studies. *Pediatric Physical Therapy,* 7 (4), 234-250.

Seaman, J.A., Corbin, C., & Pangrazi, B. (1999). Physical activity and fitness for persons with disabilities. *President's Council on Physical Fitness and Sports: Research Digest,* 3 (5), 2-9.

Shinohara, T., Suzuki, N., Oba, M., Kawasumi, M., Kimizuka, M., & Mita, K. (2002). Effects of exercise at the AT point for children with cerebral palsy. *Hospital for Joint Diseases,* 61 (1 & 2), 63-67.

Tremblay, F., Malouin, F., Richards, C.L., & Dumas, F. (1990). Effects of prolonged muscle stretch on reflex and voluntary muscle activations in children with spastic cerebral palsy. *Scandinavian Journal of Rehabilitation Medicine,* 22, 171-180.

United States Congress. (2004). P.L. 108-446 Individuals with Disabilities Education Improvement Act.

United States Department of Health and Human Services (USDHHS). (2000). *Healthy people 2010.* Rockville, MD: Office of Disease Prevention and Health Promotion.

Wolery, M., & Schuster, J.W. (1997). Instructional methods with students who have significant disabilities. *The Journal of Special Education,* 31 (1), 61-79.

World Health Organization (WHO). (2010). *Disability and rehabilitation.* www.who.int/disabilities/en/.

ABOUT THE AUTHORS

Rebecca Lytle (left) and Lindsay Canales (right).

Lindsay K. Canales, MA, has taught adapted physical education for 10 years and has 6 years of experience as an adapted physical education specialist, teaching students ranging from ages 3 to 22. She designed and implemented a PE box program, containing standards-based units and lesson plans, for eight special day classes from grades K through 8. She has also presented sessions at four annual conferences for the California Alliance for Health, Physical Education, Recreation and Dance (CAHPERD) and is a member of CAHPERD and the Northern California Adapted Physical Education Consortium. In her spare time, she enjoys watching sports and being physically active.

Rebecca K. Lytle, PhD, is a professor and chair of the department of kinesiology at California State University (CSU) at Chico. She has presented at numerous state, national, and international conferences and has received many awards, including the 2008 Professional Achievement Honor for excellence in teaching and significant contributions to the discipline from CSU Chico. She also chaired the council that received the 2007 Outstanding Council Award from the Adapted Physical Activity Council of the American Association for Physical Activity and Recreation. In 2005 she received the Recognition Award for Autism Sensory and Motor Clinic from the Autism Society of Northern California. She has numerous publications in refereed journals to her credit, and she has authored eight books or parts of books before this publication.

Lytle has served as chair of more than a dozen adapted physical education committees and councils. She is a member of many councils and organizations, including the American Alliance for Health, Physical Education, Recreation and Dance; the Council for Exceptional Children; the International Federation of Adapted Physical Activity; and the National Consortium for Physical Education and Recreation for Individuals with Disabilities. In her leisure time, she likes to hike, swim, and go on ziplines.

You'll find other outstanding
adapted physical education resources at
www.HumanKinetics.com

In the U.S. call 1.800.747.4457
Australia 08 8372 0999
Canada. 1.800.465.7301
Europe . . . . .+44 (0) 113 255 5665
New Zealand . . . 0064 9 448 1207

HUMAN KINETICS
The Information Leader in Physical Activity
P.O. Box 5076 • Champaign, IL 61825-5076